LEROS

ATHENS 2005

© Copyright 2005   MICHAEL TOUBIS EDITIONS S.A.
                      Nisiza Karela, Koropi, Attiki
                      Telephone: +30 210 6029974, Fax: +30 210 6646856
                      Web Site: http://www.toubis.gr

ISBN: 960-540-593-8

*"When shall we set sail,
when shall I sit at the helm,
To see the mounts of Leros,
and for my pain to be released"*

Traditional song

View from the castle.

CONTENTS

1. LEROS

2. MYTH AND HISTORY

3. CULTURE AND TRADITION

4. THE KASTRO

5. THE LAKKI

CONTENTS

LEROS

In times past there was an Italian soldier who would write the word Leros as "L' eros" - in other words, as love. It is quite possible that there can be no measured feelings for Leros, you either pass her by or fall completely in love with her. On this island, everything is sweetly jumbled. The blue of the Aegean with the ochre of the neo-classical houses imbued with the cosmopolitan atmosphere of Alexandria.

The geometry of the mountains with the unique architecture of the Italian buildings at Lakki, and the evening purple with the similarly-coloured patelia (volcanic rock) on the roofs of the houses, which you could say vaporises and calms the landscape below the old castle.

At Leros you might disembark carrying the baggage of notoriety – it was a place of exile

THE ISLAND OF ARTEMIS

and an island of the mad. But nature and the building fragments of history are around, to transport you to a wonderful hybrid of natural beauty and memory, which sinks within the aesthetic of the Aegean Sea that is all present.

Leros is an island for all seasons, and it does not end with the summertime apotheosis in the sea. The island is demanding, marshalling the emotions, the heart and the mind, as Leros is many things at once. It is the sea of Artemis and the myths, which have wandered in the lush green plains for thousands of years now. It is the island of the Panayia – the Virgin Mary – of Kastro - the castle - the patron saint and protector of the island, standing on the ramparts of the castle alongside the shadows of the Knights of St John.

The port of Ayia Marina.

It is the island of the sumptuous neo-classical houses of the diaspora Greeks, the excess of the merchant Greek who returns to the homeland. The styles and aesthetics of cold Odessa and warm Alexandria are here combined, spreading leisurely out over the slopes, houses with the soul of the ship owner and always with a view of the sea. It is the Malta of the Aegean, a museum of the Second World War and Lakki an Italian city built in the singular International Style. It is the island of exile, with the pitiful eyes of the saints in the wall paintings at Ayia – Saint – Kiouras, painted by the exiles at Partheni.

It is, finally, a small package of beauty, with the geological charm of its indented coastline beneath the shadow of the steep massifs that, a short drop below, disappear into small verdant plains. Because on Leros geography conspires along with history, to give the island its feminine geological form. Its countless gulfs embrace an elegant, narrow lush green centre, only 1200 metres long.

In the autumn of 1949 the academic Spyros Melas visited the Royal Technical Schools on Leros. Sipping in the taverna of Piperis at Platanos along with the high school teacher Michalis Samarakos – who has recorded this incident – Melas declared: "I find something else at Leros, something that is different from on our other islands, its light is different, its colour, its landscape with its rich alternations. How can I put it? An enchanting island, that's what she is."

1. Lerian musician playing the traditional lyre. Behind him can be seen the Kastro, with the church of the Panayia tou Kastrou built within its walls.
2. Life on Leros continues even today to unwind along the slow rhythms of island tradition.
3. Leros's architectural heritage is an important attraction for visitors during the summer months.
4. Fishing has always been one of the basic occupations of the people of Leros.
5. View from the parish church of Stavros, built in 1854. The meetings and votes of the demogerontia would take place in its courtyard.

LEROS

ARCHAGELLOS

TRIPITI

PATELIDI

STROGILLI

Korais

RADONISSIA

Agia Kioura

Plefoutis

Asfougaros

Vagia

Pano Zymi

Partheni

PARTHENI
Παρθένι

BLEFOUTIS
Βλεφούτης

VIGLIA

Agios Ioannis

Kato Zymi

KASTELI

KLIDI

+ 321

Kryphos

Artemis Temple

MARKELLOS

Agios Georgios

TOURLOTI

+ 284

Panagies

Dio Liskaria

Agios Nikolaos
Meraloudis

Kamara
Καμάρα

Aghii Saranda

ALINDA
Άλιντα

AGIA MARINA

Bourtzi

Markellos

Lia

SIKIA

Patriarcheio

KOKKALI
Κοκκάλι

AGIA MARINA
Αγία Μαρίνα

Evangelismos

Aspri Pounda

Pitiki
Πιτύκι

Agios Isidoros

KRITHONI
Κριθώνι

Christos

KASTRO

Katakrotiri

MEROBIGLI

PLATANOS
Πλάτανος

Pandeli

AGIA K

GOURNA
Γούρνα

Gournas

DRYMONAS

Bromolithos

Kefalas

DRYMONAS
Δρυμώνας

AG. THEOLOGOS

Vourlidia

Agios Georgios

Aghios Theologos

Agios
Georgios

Aghios Giorgis

Konismata

Panaghia Gourlomata

Aghios Nikolaos

LAKKI
Λακκί

Temenia
Τεμένια

TOURTOURAS

Agios Petros

MERIKIA

Location legend:

— Asphalt road

✝ Church - Monastery

▯ Archaeological site

▥ Castle

⛱ Beach

⚓ Anchorage

PATELA

Lakkiou

Lepida

TSIGOUNAS

VATHIA LAGADA

Aghios
Spyridonas

LEPIDA

Katsouni

Agystro

Panagia

Aghios Fanourios

XEROKAMBOS
Ξηρόκαμπος

Panaghia
Kavouradena

SKOUBARDA

+ 328

Xerokambou

Diap.

KATAVATI

Mavros Kavos

LEROU

DIAVLOS

MIKRO GLARONISSI

MEGALO GLARONISSI

KALYMNOS

Location

Leros is an island of the south-east archipelago that appears to act as a boundary between the windy Cyclades and the linear Dodecanese, stretched out opposite the Asia Minor coast. Administratively, Leros, along with the islets Kinaros and Levitha, comprises a Municipality within the prefecture of Kalymnos.

Leros has a territory of around 54 square km, with a maximum length of 15 kilometres and a population of 8,500.

Geography

Its highest peaks are Skoubardia, with an altitude of 328 metres in the south of the island, upon which today the rubble of the Italian military installations still stands, and Kleidi, today a military zone with an altitude of 314 metres.

Its indented coastline has a perimeter that reaches 45 km and creates large gulfs. In the north is the gulf of Partheni, the entrance of which is closed off by the islet of Archangelos, and it is approachable only for those who know the passes. In the west is the gulf of Gourna, which is not deep and has rocky islets and reefs at many points.

The little church of Ayios Isidoros is built on the largest islet, which is connected to the beach of Kokkali by a narrow pass reminiscent of Pontiko-nisi. In the south-west is the gulf of Lakki, the largest natural lake in the south-east Mediterranean. Its entrance has an opening of around 400 metres; at night, when a ship approaches, only the lighthouse on the edge shows the way. Inside the gulf are the bays of Lepidon and Temenion, as well as the cen-tral lake, which is reached by boats. To the south is the gulf of Xerokampos.

One mile separates Leros from Kalymnos with the little islands of the Glaronisia lying in between them. Divers say that there are traces of an ancient settlement lying in the depths of the sound, which it is thought may indicate the existence of a uni-fied island. The coast of Vromolithi and the fishing village of Panteli in the east form the shape of yet another gulf, with the islets of Ayia Kyriaki and Piganousa in the depths giving rosy shadows from the east. On Ayia Kyriaki stands a little church of the same name. When the weather is fine the coast of Asia Minor opposite can be seen.

In the north-east is the gulf of Ayia Marina, the island's old port, which extends out physically with successive capes towards the large beach of Alinda. Finally, past Partheni towards the north is the gulf of Plefoutis with the little island of Strongyli at its entrance.

Geology

Geologically, Leros belongs to the subpelagic zone with limestone dominating in the south part and metamorphised phyllites prevalent in the north. The constant upward and downward movements in this sensitive area have made Leros a pawn in the oddities of nature. A small, narrow sound separates it from Kalymnos and a narrow isthmus of only 1.5 km in the island's centre stops it from becoming divided into two small islands. Moreover, if the old 17th-century maps are accurate, then alluvium deposits have consolidated the mountain massif of Skoumbarda into the main body of the island. The architecture of nature has in this way bequeathed a historical heritage to the island – Lakki, the largest natural lake in the south-east Mediterranean. This is where the Italians chose to install the large aeronautical base of Gianni Rosseti, which has marked the island both historically and aesthetically.

Even its large and small calcite caves, which are lacking the usefulness of stalactite adornment, have gone down in history as Italian ammunitions stores as well as refuges for the civilian population during the Battle of Leros. In return, the island was filled with many artificial caves that the locals called "galleries", distinguishing them thus from the natural caves which are called "divine". The former were works of the Italian Engineer Corps, anti-bombardment refuges and materials storerooms during the war.

The form of the patelia, the sulphurous soil, has a characteristic purple colour with insulating qualities: In the old days they would cover their roofs with this, geology's offering to the island aesthetic.

Flora and Fauna

Leros is a small island without much variation in height over its territory. Its vegetation does not vary much then from brushwood, Mediterranean maquis (low vegetation) and limited areas of pine forests. The vegetation of Leros is heavily influenced by its climate and is thus thick, covering a large area of the island, and characterised by mossy plants and small bushes, whilst large species, such as trees and sizeable bushes, are rare. Pines, eucalyptus trees, olive trees and oaks are the trees that one meets more often. In general, the flora of Leros is dominated by those species that can survive the Mediterranean summer, whilst the island's geography, with its many hills and small but fertile valleys, creates a pleasingly alternating landscape.

As for the fauna, the main endemic species are the wild rabbit and the chukar partridge. A significant number of migrating birds also appears each year on the island, such as the blackbird, the woodcock and the thrush.

Climate

The island has a typical Mediterranean island climate, with dry, warm summers and humid winters. The great thermal capacity of the seawater prevents radical daily temperature changes. Moreover, the summer meltemi – the north or north-easterly wind – does not simply keep the weather cool, but it also cleans the coasts and keeps the waters crystal clear. Average temperature fluctuates between 20 and 26 degrees Celsius in the summer and from 12 to 17 degrees in the winter. The humid north-westerly winds that appear mainly in the winter are the cause of the rainfall, often quite intense, whilst the southerly winds are responsible for the increased humidity that, in combination with the high summer temperatures, sometimes makes the summer nights quite difficult (although, thankfully not often).

2

MYTH & HISTORY

The name

Homer sent the warriors from Calydon and other islands of the region to fight at Troy. Strabo clarifies that there may have been two Calydons, Leros and Kalymnos. Herodotus, Thucydides and a whole range of other ancient sources specifically mention the name Leros. In Byzantine times, the island was called not only Leros, but also Lernos and Lerni. Various etymological explanations are given for the origin of the name. The Lerian professor Karayiannopoulos has argued that the name comes from the flower "leirion", whilst others believe that the word means "leios", i.e. "flat". There is also the possibility that the name comes from the word Neros ("water") and the island's many waters, whilst Heysichius argued that the name came from "oleron", meaning "heavily forested".

Mythology

The 50-seater two cylinder Olympic Airways planes with the mythical names touch down at Partheni, almost right next to the traces that have been left of the temple of Iokallis Parthenos, identified as Artemis the goddess of hunting and sister of Apollo. Artemis plays a central role in the island's mythological tradition. When Oeneus was king of Calydon in Aitolia, Artemis sent over a dangerous wild boar, which destroyed the fields and terrorised the people. So Meleager, the mythical son of Oeneus and Althea decided to kill it. Artemis became very angry, considering this a personal insult, and had Meleager killed. His four sisters, Gorge, Eurymede, Deianeira and Melanippe mourned night and day, and their cries made even the wild flowers wilt. The goddess began to pity the sisters and so, by touching them with her magic wand during their sleep, transformed them into the Meleagrides - guinea hens - and transported them to the grove near the temple of Partheni so that they could forget. The guinea hens protected the temple priestesses, and neither humans nor predatory birds dared to touch them. Homer makes mention of the myth of the Meleagrides, as do Ovid in his Metamorphoses (VIII, 267) and Atheneaus in his Deipnosophistae, whilst it even inspired the tragic poets Sophocles and Euripides.

Pieces of vases, shards and obsidian blades
(Neolithic display, 3500-2800 BC,
Leros Archaeological Museum).

Prehistory

"And the writers, ancient and modern,
natives and foreigners, doubly enthusiastic,
have wonderfully written on the events
of the ancient and later fortunes of the island."
  Leriaka, *Dionysios Oikonomopoulos, 1888*

The first traces of human existence on the island
have been found in neolithic settlements as well
as at Partheni. The large quantity of unprocessed
obsidian found in around Gourna places Leros
within the western trade network that was emerg-
ing at that time in the Aegean, since the pri-
mary obsidian production centres were Melos and
Nisyros. The earliest inhabitants were the Carians,
the Leleges and the Phoenicians. Later came the
Lycians and the Eteocretans, led by the brother
of Minos Rhodamynthus and who likely used the
ports of Leros as stop-off points during their jour-
neys. The traces of Cyclopean walls at Palaiokas-
tro in Xerokampos are reminders of the island's
Mycenean past. Leros and Kalymnos participated
together in the Trojan War as the Calydonians,
under the leadership of the Heraklids Pheidippos
and Antippos. The Dorians also arrived, once they
had become dominant in Greece, to be succeeded
by the Ionians
  .

The relationship with Miletos

In his Geography, Strabo cites a testimony
of Anaximenes of Lampsacus that "The islands
of Ikaros and Leros the Milesians met at".
Herodotus even describes the commercial and
cultural exchanges between Leros and the
opposite coasts. Leros was the most southerly
of the islands – the Ionias Akron, the edge of
the Ionian – that comprised the Ionian island
periphery and gateway to Miletus. When the
tyrant Aristagoras rebelled against the Persians
and Artaphernes and Otanes marched against
him, he invited all his friends to a conference "
on what is to be done". Led by the historiographer
Hecataeus, they suggested that he flee to Leros,
which was friendly. Leros was the birthplace of
the historian Pherekydes, who lived in the first
half of the 5th century BC, mainly in Athens, and
wrote On Leros, which unfortunately does not
survive. Another child of Leros was the gnomic
philosopher and poet Demodokos.

The name of Leros appears immediately after
that of the Milesians on a marble stele inscribed
after the Persian Wars. This is a list of the allied
cities that fought under Athenian hegemony,
a defensive alliance against the Persians.

Professor Ross concluded from inscriptions,
primarily one honouring Hecataeus that he
himself found in Leros in 1842, that Leros
was not an autonomous city, but a cleruchy
(a type of colony) of Miletos. In contrast,
Professor Herold, on the basis of another stele
from the Ptolemaic period found at Partheni
– that of Aristomachos of Dromonos – believes
that Leros was autonomous with a democratic
constitution modelled on that of Athens. The
Lerians even followed the Athenian calendar,
as we can see from the date of the decree (20th
of the month Metageinion). Thucydides narrates
that when the Athenian general Phrynix was
besieging Miletus the Lerians informed him that
a large Spartan naval convoy was approaching to
put an end to the siege, and so he escaped
to Samos.

The region passed into Spartan control after the Peloponnesian War, and then to Persian control. Coins and grave steles featuring Macedonian names bear witness to the passage of the Macedonians and Alexander the Great through the island. In the region of Ayia Marina and Broutzi, most likely the old Roman garrison, arched structures and remains of an aqueduct confirm the presence of the Romans. The historical continuity of this small island, this strip of land on the sea, is impressive. Plutarch gives a characteristic piece of evidence from the period. In 74 BC Julius Caesar was kidnapped by pirates and imprisoned at Pharmaco for 32 days, until the ransom could be gathered.

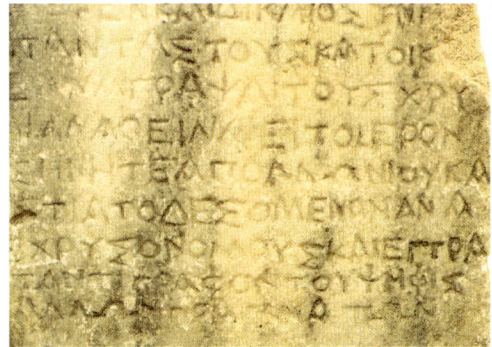

1. Honorific decree "of those residing in Leros", in honour of Aristomachos, 1st c. BC, Partheni.
2. Section of inscribed stele, 3rd-2nd c. BC, Partheni.
3. The Broutzi fortress at Ayia Marina.

Early Christian Period

Leros had not adopted Christianity by the 3rd century AD since, according to Aelian its inhabitants would not eat the Meleagrides, the guinea fowl, as they believed that they were sacred to Artemis. When Christianity did come to prevail, a three-aisled early Christian basilica was built over the temple of the Parthenos. From the end of the 3rd century AD until the early 7th century, Leros was part of the island province of the Roman Empire, part of the Asian administrative unit. Ecclesiastically, the see of Leros came under the Bishopric of Metropolitan Rhodes. The numerous early Christian basilicas, a discreet charm of the island, are representative of this period. The archaeologist Maria Michailidou has totalled eleven: at Partheni, Ayia Varvara, Ayioi Saranda, the site of Xenona, Panayies at Elinda, Ayios Ioannis Theologos (St John the Evangelist), Ayios Nikolaos at Xerokampos, Ai Yiannis at Fakoudia, Ayios Petros and Ayios Nikitas at Drymonas. The Diocese of Leros was founded at that time, and definitely before AD 553, as the Bishop of Leros John took part in the Fifth Ecumenical Synod. The cast of the bull "John, Humble Bishop of Leros" can today be found in the Archaeological Museum.

1. Small amphora, base of a skyphos vase, skyphos with inscribed circles and a hytra with an inscription, from the basilica at Partheni (11th-13th c. AD, Leros Archaeological Museum).
2. Asia Minor and African style lamps, from the basilica at Partheni (4th-5th c. AD, Leros Archaeological Museum).
3. Section of a small column with a Corinthian capital and a two-pointed double column window divider from the basilica at Partheni (6th c. AD, Leros Archaeological Museum).
4. Bronze Byzantine coins, from the secular building at Partheni (AD 575, Leros Archaeological Museum).
5. The early Christian basilica at Partheni, 5th-6th c. AD.

The Blessed Christodoulos at Leros

In June of 1087 the Emperor Alexios I Komnenos granted Patmos, Lipsi and part of Leros to John Latrinos, later the Blessed Christodoulos, by issue of a bull. The parts of Leros were the suburbs of Partheni and Temenion and the walls and buildings located within the inner surround wall of the Castle. Christodoulos reached Patmos first and then went on to Leros. According to evidence provided by Manuel Gedeon, the Lerian medieval scholar, Christodoulos built a small church and the dependency of Ayios Georgios at Partheni using pieces of the columns of the ancient temple. The Lerians were opposed to this decision, and they threatened Christodoulos and the monks. This, combined with pressure from his mother Anna

Dalassini, forced the Emperor to issue a new bull granting the whole of the castle to the monks, whilst at the same time giving the locals the castle of Lepidon and transferring the town there. This is where, according to D. Oikonomopoulos's Leriaka, *it was to remain "throughout the whole period of the Frankish occupation of the island until its conquest by the Turks in 1523".*

The imperial bull as well as the proceedings of the transfer as drawn up by the notary John Antzas are today kept in the Archive of the Monastery of Patmos (ten documents in total). The monks built many churches during the period in which they controlled the island. These include Ayios Theologos at Lakki, Ayios Zacharias at Merikia, and Panayia Gourlomata and Ayios Georgios at Drymonas..

The era of the Knights of St John

In 1309 the Knights of St John, otherwise known as the Knights Hospitaller or the Knights of Rhodes, took over Leros. The Knights did not have enough resources to keep the islands that they themselves called the "Scattered (sporades) islands", and so they installed a garrison leader at the head and employed local residents as guards. Along with Kalymnos and Nisyros, Leros came under the administration of Kos. During the period of their rule, the Knights of St John created new fortress works on the castle so as to adapt to the era of cannon fire. This is when the third surround wall was constructed, in which we can still see embedded coats of arms, as well as the tower that protects the castle gate. Leros was a focal point of the competition between the Turks and the Knights for control of the Aegean Sea.

In 1477 Leros was subject to a fierce Turkish attack during Mohammed's campaign against Rhodes. There were further raids in 1502, when Leros was besieged by 18 ships and in 1505 when Kemal Reis failed to conquer Rhodes. In 1508 Kemal Reis, with 20 ships, 4000 soldiers, 26 ladders, 4 canons and 4 bombardas again besieged the castle for four days, yet with no result. The constant raids and pillaging meant that the island was eventually abandoned by its population. The cartographer Piri Reis characteristically described Leros as a "barren island".

On 24 December of 1522 the hand-over of the islands was signed between Suleyman the Magnificent and the Magister of the Knights. Finally, the garrison of Leros was also handed over after being besieged in January 1523.

Days of the Ottoman Empire

The residents of the small islands sent representatives to Suleyman so as to declare their allegiance to him. They offered him fresh bread and sponges, their only products as they told him, pointing to their destitute land and lack of water. As a result, Suleyman granted the privilege of complete self-government and autonomy to all the islands with a firman, or decree. Rhodes and Kos, however, were excluded from these privileges. The islands were named the "Privileged Sporades" and they paid a maktu tax in two instalments and which varied for each island. Each island was governed by local notables, the mayor and the demogerontes (a council of "elders") who were elected in the first week of each year. The Sultan was represented by a sumbasi who did not interfere in internal affairs.

During the Ottoman occupation the main bulk of the population was transferred to the area around the castle.

In 1648, during the Turkish-Venetian war, Leonardo Foscolo bombarded the Castle from the port of Ayia Marina, destroying a portion of the wall and becoming lord of the island for a brief spell. Leros enjoyed a period of growth and prosperity after the final victory of the Turks over the Venetians and the relative calm that prevailed with full Turkish domination of the Aegean. The population increased, trade and shipping expanded, important personages emerged. It is not by chance, then, that only a year after the decisive prevalence of the Ottomans the formal opening of the restored church of the Panayia of the Kastro was held.

During the 18th century a series of high clerics from Leros, five in total, became Bishops of Herakleia in Thrace, the first being Gennadios in 1714 and the last being Ignatius Staraveros. In 1726 the famous school of the Panayia of Kastros was opened by the monk Damascenos. The school had around 20 pupils who were taught subjects ranging from basic literacy to theology for the most advanced. The school acquired a large number of manuscripts and books through donations, thus raising its standards. Unfortunately, many of these are no longer surviving today.

Leros, water painting, Gennadios Library, Athens. From the manuscript of Christophoro Buondelmonti's Libro de le insule de lo archipelago.

The Revolution of 1821

Despite its privileged status Leros was to rebel along with the other islands during the revolution of 1821, after the letter that was sent from the Patriarch of Alexandria Theophilos Pankostas to the Bishop of Lerni Jeremiah on 27 March 1821. Krasouzis Tourkomanolos and the Hadzimanolis brothers took a leading role in the uprising. On 29 August 1824, a Friday, the naval battle of Gerontas took place opposite Leros. The residents observed the battle from the mountains and watched Vatikiotis, the Hydraiot captain of the fireship bombard the Tunisian frigate with 38 cannons and the Turkish-Egyptian fleet withdraw to Kos.

Leros was part of the Greek state from 1821 to 1830. Ioannis Capodistrias appointed a Commissioner Extraordinary for the Eastern Sporades, of which constituency Leros was also part. Markos Reisis, mayor of Leros, officially raised the Greek flag. Documents issued in Leros at that time were issued in the name of the Hellenic Polity and the Governor, with a stamp bearing armed Athena and the title "Wrath of War". Ultimately, however, with the Protocol of London signed on 3/2/1830, the protecting powers granted the Dodecanese and Samos to the Turks. In 1835, the reformist Sultan Mahmud II reinstated the islands' privileges with a firman, on the proposal of representatives of the Tetranese, the "Four Islands" (Leros, Patmos, Ikaria and Kalymnos). The representative of Leros was Ioannis Gedeon, the father of Manuel.

With the outbreak of the Cretan revolution in 1867, however, Turkey asked that these privileges be abolished. Finally, on the intervention of England, the institution of the demogerontes was kept, although a kaymakam was appointed as governor of the island. The limitations on the autonomy of the islands were increased with the installation of the Turkish employees in the Customs Houses, the Port Authorities and for the issuing of passports. From the 8% tax collected by Customs, 3% remained on the islands. In the Diary of the Prefecture of the Archipelago, published by the Prefecture in 1886, Leros, with 4,000 inhabitants, was under a separate administration, that of the Prefecture of Chios, which included the province of Patmos and the islands of Lipsi, Fournoi and Femaina. The governor was Reouf Bey and the local council had a mixed composition of Greeks and Turks. In a decree dated 13th August 1894, the demogerontes refused to hand over the seals of the Common Customs to the Local Council of Chios, reminding the latter that they did not have such a right since Leros was governed by a kaymakam and was not a province.

With the Young Turk revolution in Turkey in 1908, and the modernisation of the state, it was requested that the Dodecanese be ranked equal to the other Turkish provinces. In March 1910, the privileges were abolished on the order of the Sublime Porte. A new decree on 28 April, however, cancelled the previous one, although requesting compulsory military conscription.

Italian Occupation

On 13 May of 1912, a Sunday and also May Day in keeping with the old Gregorian calendar still in use then, the fishermen of Panteli witnessed three Italian battle ships – the San Giorgio, the Regina Margarita and the Regina Elena - drop anchor. At Ayia Marina, the marines disembarked from the cruiser Piza. The Turkish garrison, 22 people in all, was handed over and the Italians at Platano, cheered on by the people, raised the tri-coloured flag of the Kingdom of Italy. At a meeting of the representatives of all the islands at Patmos in June 1912, the complete autonomy of all the islands as the "Polity of the Aegean" was declared. Leros was represented by the schoolmaster Ioannis Abelas. On 6 January 1916, Papanastasis raised the Greek flag and was subsequently jailed for two months. At the instigation of Eleftherios Venizelos, the Dodecanese Committee was founded, led by Skevos Zervos from Kalymnos and Paris Roussos from Leros.

Temporary Italian control over the Dodecanese, which officially were still a Turkish province and Greek for a year with the Venizelos-Titoni agreement, became permanent with the Treaty of Lausanne in 1923. Article 15 stipulated that the islands were to remain in the hands of the Italians. The islands would constitute a Possedimonto (possession) and not a Colonia (colony), administered by the Foreign Ministry and not the Ministry for Colonies, under the name Isole Italiane dell Egeo. Italian rule continued until 1943.

In May 1923 the plans for the transformation of the Lakki gulf into a great aeronautical base kicked off. The Italian King Vittore Emmanuel visited Leros on 29 May. The interventions to the landscape were dramatic. The mountains were filled with batteries and military facilities, in particular after

The bust of Papanstasis (Archimandrate Anastasios, N. Zafeiropoulos).

1936 when a large section of the island became a military zone and was closed off with barbed wire. Ramblers can discover many of these facilities scattered around the mountains, with their impressive wall paintings today. This was when the central axial road, lined with eucalyptus trees and which connects the whole of the island even today, was constructed. A modern new town with impressive buildings and infrastructure on the International Style of architecture was created at Lakki. At the same time, a programme of "Italianisation" was begun, the main targets being the churches, which they attempted to detach from the Orthodox Ecumenical Patriarchate in Constantinople with the excuse that they would become autonomous and for educational purposes.

With the replacement of Mario Lago by Devecci in 1936, the measures became more austere. The ordination of new priests was forbidden and appointments of new Bishops had to be ratified by the Italians. This was also when the Elementary School was built at Lakki, in which Catholic nuns taught, whilst an attempt was made to downgrade the High School, using financial problems as an excuse. Parisis Bellenis offered to cover the costs himself, but the Italians declined the offer. In the school year 1934-35 the High School was downgraded to a "sub-High School", functioning with only one class until 1936, finally being closed in 1937. Finally, in February 1937 Devecci abolished the institution of the demogerontia, replacing it with elected mayors and appointed podesta.

On 25 July 1943, Mussolini was removed from power, with General Bandolino taking over the running of the Italian government, which announced Italy's surrender. Italy changed camps and became an ally of the British.

1. *Seal of the Demogerontia, 1828*
   (General State Archives - Regional Archive of Leros).
2. *Document of the Demogerontia, 1910*
   (General State Archives - Regional Archive of Leros).
3. *Document of the Government of the Italian*
   Islands of the Aegean, Portolago
   (General State Archives - Regional Archive of Leros).

The battle of Leros

The Germans did not waste any time, occupying Rhodes on 11 September and Kos a little later. Along with the airports of these islands, they became masters of the skies over the Aegean. The British reached Leros gradually, and organised the defence of the island along with the Italians, albeit within an atmosphere of suspicion.

On 26 September 1943, German planes sunk the legendary Greek destroyer the Queen Olga and the British destroyer the HMS Intrepid along with it. From that day, German bombardments took place on a daily basis, aiming to destroy the batteries. There were 984 raids between 26 September and 11 November, which dropped 1,096 tons of bombs. Leros was defended by 8,000 Italian and 3,000 British troops, with 26 batteries. Head of the British forces was Commander Tinley and the Italians were led by Admiral Mascherpa. The Germans, knowing the blind spots of the island's defence, prepared to land. The residents hid in caves to escape the bombs.

On the night of the 11th to the 12th of November 1943, the German landing began. The German landing forces were intercepted at Gourna and Plefoutis by the batteries, but they managed to land at dawn and to set up beachheads at Pityki, Panayies and Ano Zymi. At midday, German parachutists fell at Rachi, with dire losses, cutting the island in two.

Finally, after a combined attack from air and sea with ferocious clashes, sometimes man to man, the Germans overcame the defence of the Italians and the British and took over the island at one minute to 12 on 16 November. The British cemetery at Alinda, with its 187 graves, is a reminder of that battle. The Germans abolished the Italian mayor, and the elections that were held on 24 February 1945 were won by S. Angelou, who

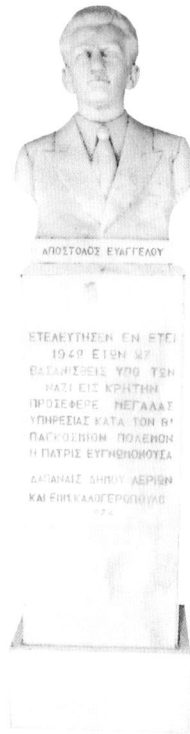

The bust of Apostolos Evangelos.

took over as mayor on 12 March. The Greek school had opened once more on 3rd January.

Incorporation

On 8 May 1945 Germany surrendered without conditions, and on the same day at Symi General Otto Wangener handed over the Dodecanese to the Allies. A British Military Administration was thus installed in the Dodecanese.

Archbishop Damasecenos visited Rhodes on 15 May. On 12 February 1947 the decision of the Paris Conference was announced, by which the Dodecanese were given to Greece. On 31 March the Union Jack was lowered on all the islands and the Greek flag raised in its place.

At Platanos, decorated with flags, the British Commander read out the protocol with which the islands of Leros, Patmos, Lipsi, Arkioi, Levitha and Pharmaco were handed over to the Greek Military Administration, represented by Lieutenant Georgantas. At five minutes to 12 they ascended to the Town Hall, and at 12 o'clock precisely the Union Jack was replaced by the Greek flag on the building's flagpole, to the great cries of joy of the crowds of people who had gathered from all over the island, and where it has remained ever since.

On 31 March 1947 Admiral Ioannides took over the administration of the islands with a law passed in the Greek Parliament foreseeing their incorporation into Greece on 7 March 1948. The long occupation of the Dodecanese had ended once and for all.

The Italian military facilities on the island, however, were still to determine the future of the island after the war. In 1949, the Italian barracks housed the Royal Technical Schools and in 1957 they became home to the PIKPA psychiatric hospital, receptacle of human pain from throughout Greece. The military dictatorship of 1967-1974 would send its political prisoners to two buildings at Lakki and Partheni.

Along with Halicarnassus, Oropos and Korydallos, Partheni was immortalised in Mikis Theodorakis's resistance ode. Who knows, that "cyclamen in the rock's crack" might even be the same one that sprouts in the rubble of the wall of the temple of Ilokalis Parthenos.

Because the history of this island has never fallen into a slumber…

1. Monument of the destroyer Queen Olga at Lakki.
2. Monument of the Sacred Band at Lakki.

3

CULTURE & TRADITION

Customs and traditions

Customs and traditions may today slowly be disappearing from daily life, with the televisual organisation of free time and the dominance of the entertainment industry. Island Greece, however, is still resistant and resolute. The traditions and events described below, then, may not be so prevalent in daily life anymore, but they are still preserved in our era.

On the **celebration of the Epiphany,** with icons and hexapters borne aloft, the priest throws the Cross into the sea – a maritime custom – whilst the church bells ring and the ships blow their horns. The diver who catches the Cross becomes the hero of the day, having the right to place the Cross on a disk and collect money in it. The custom is followed in the coastal parishes of Xerokampos, Lakki and Ayia Marina. During the **Apokries** (the pre-Lenten carnival), a large carnival party is organised in which the whole island participates. Dressed in costume, which the locals call "kamoutzeles", celebrants tour the houses and lanes making jokes and calling out improvised lyrics. The little children who, trained by their parents, would go around satirising people and situations were also called "kamoutzeles" or "kalogerakia". Today, however, the term has come to mean all those who dress up in costume.

On **1 March** the children entwine a red and a white thread together and tie it around one of their fingers so that the sun will not burn them, removing it at Easter time. In the old days, they would burn it in the oven that was roasting the special Easter bread made with chickpea flour.

During **Holy Week** the floors of the churches are laid with aromatic wild flowers and hemp. Their fragrance is released by the treading of the church-goers and combines with the aroma of the incense to create a strange aromatic communion that matches perfectly with the religious hymns being sung. On the morning of Good Friday, the faithful place a little vinegar in their mouths, in the same way that Christ was sprinkled. The procession with the Epitaph is glorious. The **Resurrection** is noisy and home-made firecrackers are thrown, with the parish of Christos playing a leading role. The downside is that the firecrackers have spread uncontrollably throughout the whole of Holy Week. During the Second Resurrection, "they burn Judas", i.e. an effigy of Judas made from old clothes and straw on which they hang firecrackers and triangles. With the cries of "Christ is Risen" the Judas is set fire to. On the morning of the Ascension they would put in a corner of the yard a piece of incense in a glass of water with a candle lit for Christ as He ascended to heaven. On the same day the children would start swimming in the sea, convinced that they would not get cold. This continues until today, although they perhaps no longer utter the same words as they jump in: "Christ Ascends, I ascend to a dive in the sea".

The **feast of Kledon**, a remnant from ancient divination, is held on 24 June on the feast day of St John the Baptist, when they light great fires and burn the May Day wreaths as well as the palms and myrrh from the Epitaph. On this day the unmarried women pour "unspoken" water into a jug (i.e. water that they brought from the spring without speaking to anyone) along with "simadia" or "rizikaria" (personal effects such as rings, pins and earrings). They cover the jug with a red cloth whilst singing "We lock Kledon up with the joy of Ai Yiannis, and whichever girl has good a good riziko (fate) should give over to take it." The jug remained covered and in the open beneath the stars all night long, being opened only at sunrise. They would remove the objects one by one, accompanying each item with a couplet that was believed to divine the fortune of its owner. The girls would wash their faces with the "unspoken" water, and the first unmarried man they would meet after stepping out of their houses was thought to be their future husband.

The most important religious festival was the walk as far as the castle on the **feast day of the Panayia of the Kastro**. This is still continued today, and is evolving into a pilgrimage. On the eve of 14 August, during the first hours after noon, the church bell begins to ring and people come from all the corners of the island dressed in their Sunday best. They form a stunning human line of locals and visitors that begins at Platano and stretches out over 500 steps as far as the castle gate, being continuously

replenished until late in the evening. The view from afar is amazing, as the whitewashed steps contrast with the grey rock and with the blue background of the sky. It is characteristic that among the crowds are many non-Orthodox foreigners, who unknowingly have become part of the tradition originating from when the Turks and Catholics of the island would also come to pay their respects.

Another strong custom that is observed today is the **Lerian wedding**. The preparations for the wedding begin several days earlier with a general recruitment at the bride's house. They prepare the sweets, the poungia ("bites") and home-made drinks, such as the soumada almond drink. The bed is laid on the Thursday evening by unmarried friends of the bride, whilst they sing the pastika bridal songs. The guests wish the couple well and throw rice on the bed along with sweets and, most of all, money for good luck and happiness. At the end they throw a small boy onto the bed so that the firstborn will be a boy, "the successor".

On the day of the wedding the bride's friends dress her and write their names on the soles of her shoes. Whichever girl's name has been erased by the end of the service will be the one to marry next. At the same time, in the groom's house, he too is getting prepared amongst his friends, who tease him with pastika couplets. The bridal procession starts off from the bride's house in the direction of that of the groom. In the front are some girls who hold gifts and, symbolically, honey, sweets and wine. When the families unite they all set off together for the church, to the accompaniment of music played by local musicians and everyone joins in the singing. After the church service, and just as throughout the whole of Greece, the traditional partying begins, often lasting until well into the early hours.

There are many other customs from everyday life. When there are storms at sea, girls whose sweethearts or brothers work on the boats go to the church of Ai-Nikolas (St Nicholas) and sweep.

1. Fire at the feast of Ai Yiannis (St John) the Evangelist.
2. Eve of the celebration of the Dormition of the Virgin on 15 August at the Panayia tou Kastrou.
3. Celebration on the castle.

They then throw the sweepings into the sea so that it calms down. This is known as frokalizoun, from the frokala, i.e the sweepings. In order to sweeten the sea for their journeys, sailors would rub sesame-honey, sisamomelo, into their anchor and oars. When a baby was born, perhaps because the parents did not trust the disorganised official records, they would write the date of the birth on the back of their icons. They would slaughter a rooster in the foundations of a house. When somebody is celebrating his or her name day they pull their ears. When something has been lost, and also when they want to make something appear, they make pies called fanouropites (from "fano", to show). These are made from seven or nine different ingredients, and they make a wish as they prepare them. The fanouropites are then shared throughout the neighbourhood.

The open-air festivals and the feasting that accompanied them have declined today, and they are now held at night clubs and restaurants. The last of the festivals, and also the most important, which is slowly dying out, is that of the Panayia in the square at Platano. The folk musicians would greet the pilgrims who came down from the castles, and they in their turn would share in the partying that went on all night. On the initiative of the local authority, a festival takes place every summer at Alonari in July, and the "Wine Festival" is held in August at Xerokampos. Finally, since August 1997, the popular "Alindia" Water Sports Games are held each summer at Alinda, including almost every sport related to water, such as rowing, diving and swimming.

1. Student procession at Lakki.
2. Start of the yacht race at Lakki.
3. Procession of the icon of Ayia Marina into the alleys of Ayia Marina.
4. Moment from the "Alindia" Water Sports Games.

4

Music and dances of Leros

"On Leros, day breaks and sun sets with songs.
It is with songs that the sun rises, and with them
that it disappears again. One tune follows another
and all together welcome life as though it is
a boat that comes and goes, that comes once
more and leaves again."

Leros's songs, T. Moraitis

The songs of Leros became wider known in 1938
when Stamatis Hadjidakis played them on Greek
Public Radio. Later, the well-known singing sisters Amelia and Dikaia Hadjidaki continued their
family's musical tradition by recording and singing
Lerian tunes throughout the world. Characteristic
songs of theirs are "When shall we set sail", "My little
sea", "My three-sailed ship" and "My dearest".

The songs of Leros are improvisations, varia-
tions on an original tune, the havas, over which
the next lyrics are added. The instrumentalist was
always ready to kick off the party with a small
group, which gradually grew and then new songs
would jump out during the night's wine drinking.
They would end up in a house with the table song
"The song of dawn", waiting for the rooster to broil
before going to bed or starting the revelry anew.
"A little bird was crying sadly at dawn, because his
heart was full of pain and his wing broken."

The havades (plu.) were improvised melodies
that came to be completed over time following the
traditional technique. They are tunes to be sung
whilst seated according to the living room, and
slow songs of the land. They bear the names of the
old musicians who were the first to inspire them,
or of revellers who favoured particular tunes and
would sing them constantly. Typical havades are
those of Yiannoukas, better known as the havas of
Konstantis, of whom it is said that when he sang at
Ayia Paraskevi they could hear him at Vromolitho:

"Aide; my eyes I cannot
raise up high
aide, my pained heart
I cannot console."

The havas of Loulourgas:

"Like a partridge you pace over the land,
like a pigeon you run,
shame on the most beautiful,
and a mismatch for you not to have

The havas of Bilalis:

"Achi, I want to be the perfume
that you put in your hair
achi, and with your every breath
I would enter your heart."

The best known of all the havades is the havas
of Brouzos. Brouzos was the captain of a brazzera
(a three-sailed ship) and he would often sail to the
orient. There would be a festival on his return, with
non-stop partying for three days and nights.

"Brouzos has gone to drop anchor
and the weather won't settle down.
Oh, my Lerian Panayia
who is on the upper castle
help me, the poor man.
and I shall bring you bread"

Typical songs are the peismatika ("stubborn
songs") and the pastika. With the xanastrefa of
peismatika songs, the Lerians satirise others and
themselves. These scoffing songs are "to be heard"
by someone and they will "decorate" someone,
sung to the accompaniment of the bagpipes.

"Down on the beach, on the sand
the boats are having a wedding
they invited the aga
to fry the eggs
they invited the master
to fry the liver."

The pastika are the songs that are sung as
part of the wedding preparations, and they are a
continuation of the ancient wedding songs that
are sung even today, since many weddings still
follow the traditional ritual.

- "My groom, do not spin your pistol too much,
because our bride is young and you frighten her."

- Neighbourhood women from above and below, we took your groom and you all sat down."
- "Come down, Kyra Panayia with your only child and give your blessings to the couple that shall be born."

The traditional songs of Leros have been released on a double CD accompanied by a 135-page booklet, entitled "The Songs of Leros" ("Tis Leros ta Tragoudia"). The recordings are by traditional musicians and singers and it is published by the Artemis Youth Educational Association of Leros ("Morphotikos Syllogos Neon Lerou Artemis"). The Musical Folk Archive helped in the production of the CD, which was put together by leading Greek musicologists Markos Dragoumis and Thanasis Moraitis.

Musical Instruments

In the local dialect, musical instruments are known as paigndia ("games"). The basic instruments are the santouri (dulcimer), the tsabouna (bagpipes), the lyre, the laouto (lute) and the fiddle. The santouri belongs to the stringed percussion group of musical instruments. It is a "polyphonic" instrument that is used in improvisation, but also as an accompaniment. In contrast with mainland Greece, on the Aegean islands the santouri is mainly played using only one melody. It has a trapezoid shape, three metal cords are stretched for each musical phoneme, and they are played using two small sticks.

The tsabouna is a traditional herding instrument, similar in appearance to the gaida (another type of bagpipe). It is made up of one bag made from animal leather, into which the player blows air with a specially adapted mouthpiece. In the lower section there is a pipe with eight holes. By making the appropriate movements, the musician exerts pressure on the bag beneath their armpit, opening and closing the holes on the pipe with their fingers.

The island lyre is a pear-shaped instrument that is usually played on its own, accompanied only by the rhythmic foot-tapping of the player on the ground. It is made from wood and a bow is used. The laouto is also a stringed instrument, and its name comes from the Arab word al-ud. Its sound-box has the shape of a half-pear and is made from thin, curved strips of wood. The chords are located on the flat top surface, the number of which is also determined by the width of the instrument.

In the traditional musical bands of Leros, these instruments appear in the following three combinations: 1. santouri – fiddle – lute; 2. santouri – fiddle; 3. tsabouna – lyre.

Traditional musicians of Leros.

Dances

The traditional dances of Leros are circle dances, a reflection of the collective community life. They are distinguished into slow and lively or "jumping" dances. As soon as the party gets going, and to the tune of the instruments, the kavos kicks off, i.e. the head of the dance who is followed by everyone else. Characteristic dances are:

The Lerikos has two versions: the isos, which is a slow dance with a light sway and the stavrotos, during which the dancers hold on to each other with crossed arms. The Pasoumaki, which is similar to the stavrototos, is danced with the tips of the toes. There is also a Lerian syrtos (a circle dance with nine steps forward and three back), which is similar to the classic island syrtos and the bucolic sousta (swing) or stoumbikti, so called from the leg movements. The balaristos is a jumping dance, which the Byzantines called the skirto (jump) according to Athina Tarsouli, because the dancers appear to jump in surprise.

Dances from other islands, for example Rhodes and Kos and the balos dance (danced by a couple) arealso danced on Leros. The karsilamas (fast dance for couples) and the zeibekiko (solo dance) have come from the nearby Asia Minor coast. A characteristic dance, which is no longer practised, is the "dance of the broom". Five or six couples would participate, and the man at the end of the circle would hold a broom instead of a female dancing partner. As they turned, the dancers would let go of each other's hands and exchange dancing partners. The man who didn't manage to find a partner would be handed the broom. The visitor has the chance to see all these dances at the many revels on the island and also at the Artemis Educational Association's annual event each summer.

The local idiom

Although school Greek is today becoming increasingly dominant among the younger generations, the traditional Lerian idiom, with references to the Attic dialect, often enters general daily speech. In the neighbourhoods, the villages, the trawler boats and some small

coffee houses, the visitor who goes off the beaten tourist track will be able to hear this language leaping tirelessly out, like a murmur with a sing-song tone, as though it were following the playing of the waves. Enjoy the bliss of ancient island chatter.

The linguistic idiom of the Lerians is pure Greek, and it represents the evolution of the Attic dialect over time, as this was shaped on the islands and in Ionia. For example, the Lerians say "ifaga" as opposed to "efaga" (I ate), "olos" as opposed to "tholos" (hazy), "kioura" as opposed to "kyra" (lady). They also adopt the Aeolic dialect in some instances, for example "plevgo" as opposed to "pleo" (to float). The Lerian dialect has that lilting characteristic shared by all the residents of the islands of southern Greece and Cyprus. It also features the pronunciation of the final –n along, whilst the initial beta (β), pi (π) and kappa (κ) sound like the Latin b, d and g, for example "a-dychi" as opposed to "an tyhci" (if it chances) and "e-gamnei" as opposed to "dhen kamnei" (it won't do).

The letter chi (χ) is often pronounced like the English "sh", e.g. "sheri" as opposed to "heri" (hand) and "shoiros" as opposed to "choiros" (pig).

The final –zi or –zei is pronounced –tzi or –tzei, e.g. "agiatzi" (to bless), "potizei" (to water), "myritzei" (to smell). The theta (θ) is pronounced as a "t" sound, e.g. "peteros" as opposed to "petheros" (father-in-law). The ending –ia has a heavy pronunciation, e.g. "kleidargia" as opposed to "kleidargi-a" (lock) and "parigioria" as opposed to "parigori-a" (consolation). The ending –ne is added to the aorist for almost all verbs in the first person plural, e.g. "fagame-ne" as opposed to "fagame" (we ate), "kathisam-ne" as opposed to "kathisame" (we sat). Characteristic is the preservation of the ancient Greek double consonant with a particularly heavy pronunciation in the spoken word, e.g. "kokkalo" (bone), as well as the conversion of the double –ss to –ts, e.g. "thalassa" (sea) becomes "thalatsa".

A group of dancers from the "Panhellenic Union of Lerians".

Lerian costume

The islanders' dress code is today quite different from what it was in the past. Aside from the black caps still worn by some fishermen and the head-scarves of the old women, modern styles and fashions have taken over. In what follows we describe the traditional Lerian costume for all those interested in the island's folk art.

Male costume was simple. A black vraka (breeches), short waistcoat, red fez with a tassel and belt. By contrast, women's costume was richly decorated. On their heads they wore a fine yellow tseberi headscarf with little flowers. Their inner garments consisted of a woven silk shift with wide sleeves and an underskirt. Over this was a top shirt (anteri) open at the sides, and a long-sleeved bodice with broad sleeves that were folded over to expose the embroidery of the shift. The libades was a short felt pelisse with gold embroidery at the edges. There was a second type of costume worn under the top shirt, through which the batzakia (legs) of the breeches could be seen. A kazaka (jumper-blouse) with a frill (frambalas) was worn over the underskirt. Around their waists they wore a large multi-coloured kerchief known as the kolozostis (bottom belt!), and there was also a difference in the way the kerchief was tied. Around their necks and over their chests they hung gold chains with Venetian coins and pendants. The girls wove their own woollen socks, and women's shoes were dark and flat.

1. Members of the lerian association "Artemis", wearing traditional clothes.
2. Dancers from the "Panhellenic Union of Lerians".

Local cuisine

The local cuisine has the typical Mediterranean island diet at its base, with some influences from oriental cooking that were most likely brought over by the refugees who reached the island from the neighbouring Asia Minor coast. In any case, the close relations between the two areas go back a long way.

There are a number of local specialities. The Lerian tyropitta (cheese pie) is made with fresh myzithra (cream cheese) in a special shape, and it is particularly tasty. One can find it at all the island's bakeries.

The poungia (bite-sized) sweets have a special filling made from bitter almonds in dough sprinkled with caster sugar. You can find them at patisseries or even put in an order. Special fruits of Leros are tropical fruits such as the lotus and the gavafes with their strange tastes, and fruits that the Lerians of Egypt may have brought with them, such as the frangosyko fig.

Other specialities are the salted mackerel, which is sold in jars, as well as cleaned "bubbles" (pieces of squid), the soumada almond drink, the diasogalo (similar to soumada) and the xerotigana (dry fries). One special flavour that is common in the homes is the combination of pastas with pulses. Koukouvades are plaited round bread rolls with a red egg in the centre, which is considered to be a gift from the mother-in-law.

Generally speaking, one can eat very well in Leros, and relatively cheaply too, whilst each restaurant has its own special recipes. Traditional products such as honey, myzithra with a hint of must, capers, oregano, savory and herbs that the lately departed "Votanos" (herb man) would sell in the street can now be found in a shop at Platano, whilst the sweets are available in a patisserie at Ayia Marina.

Traditional Easter goodies of Leros.

Occupations of the inhabitants

The occupations of the inhabitants of Leros are similar to those of the residents of all the other Aegean islands. So, the people of the hamlets of Panteli and Xerokampos work in fishing, whilst there are fish farms at Lakki and Partheni. There are also small units of cultivation scattered throughout the countryside, and in a more organised fashion in the two greenhouses. Livestock is reared with free-range herds, which are unfortunately not controlled, whilst there is a unit for cattle husbandry. A large section of the population works in tourism during the summer months. The growth in tourism has led to an increase in construction work and related economic activities.

Of the main occupations of the people of Leros, farming and bee keeping have always been a mainstay, alongside fishing and, more recently, tourism.

Even so, the main element in local economic activity are the services of the State Infirmary, which employs over 1,000 people whilst hospital demand for supplies strengthens many local businesses.

At Leros one can see, even today, traditional professions that have almost been lost. It is impressive that the work is carried out using the same methods and tools that have been used for centuries.

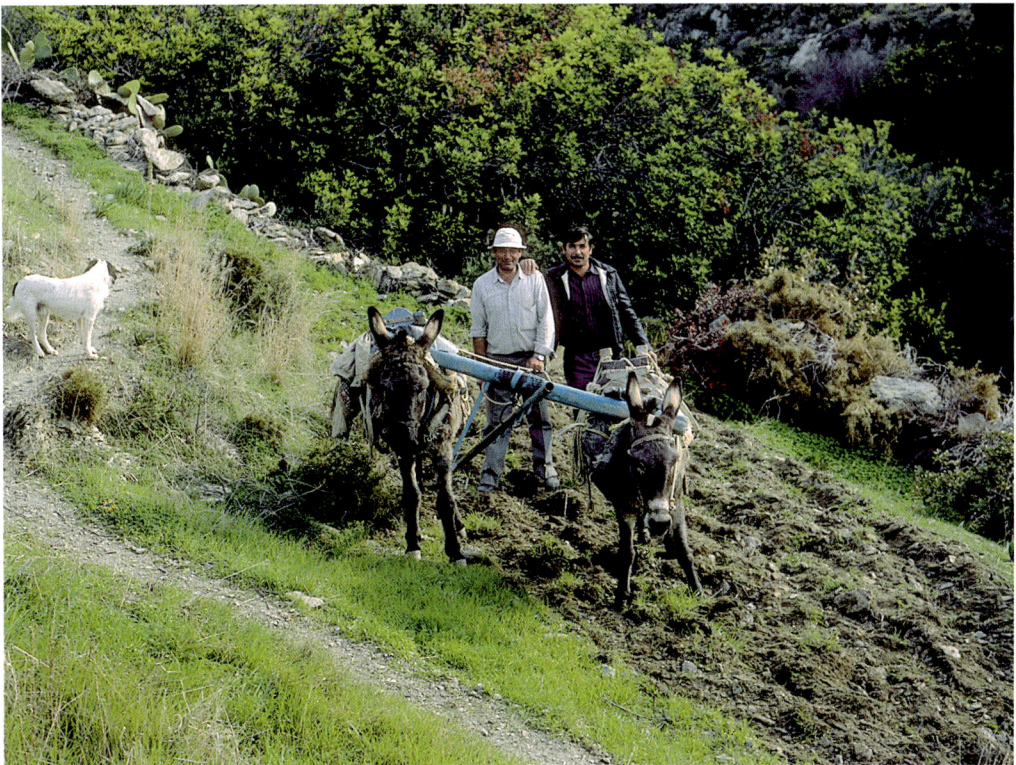

Architecture - Town planning

"The architectural physiognomy of the island is equally unique. Local popular architecture of mainly the previous centuries mixes with the foreign urban trends of the day. Next to the popular architectural traditions, then, the civic character of the buildings and complexes is also important, particularly the existence of a town plan during the years of Italian rule."

Traditional Greek Architecture - Leros
Marina Veniadou

Characteristic neo-classical houses at Ayia Marina.

One of the most exciting aspects of town planning is that of creation, with the development and, above all, the movement of towns and villages in the limited space of the islands. History comes along to knock down that which geography has decided, and the towns and villages come and go throughout space and time.

Partheni, with the closed sea, protected completely from the north by the island of Archangelo, and its fertile plain, may very likely have been the earliest settlement core. This appears to have been confirmed in 1979 with the discovery of neolithic pottery and shards. The evolution of communications and military

technology increased the threats that could come by sea and the low fortress at Partheni did not suffice. The pottery that was brought to light, not by the archaeologist's trowel but by workers opening up a ditch at the port of Ayia Marina, as well as the Cyclopean masonry in the walls of the Castle are signs that the primary archaic settlement was later located at Ayia Marina. Archaic building activity, however, can also be found in the south of the island, at Palaiokastro and Xerokampos. This is evident from the remains of the Cyclopean walls and traces of an ancient signalling station that is contemporary with the one at Partheni.

1. *The pyrgospito at Ayios Theologos (17th-18th c.) at Lakki.*
2. *Traditional house at Christos.*
3. *Wall painting at the house of Madame Zabeta Christodoulou at Christos.*
4. *Characteristic example of a pebbled yard.*

In 1087, when the Byzantine Emperor Alexios Komnenos granted part of Leros to the Blessed Christodoulos a battle broke out between the monks and the residents. An agreement was reached through the help of the Emperor's mother. The residents, and the main settlement along with them, moved from the Castle of the Lepides and, according to Gedeon, remained there until the Turkish conquest of the island. Around the same time, another medieval centre developed within and around the Kastro, as far as the port of Ayia Marina. In addition to the castles, the island's medieval architectural remains include the pyrgakia. These are small towers (pyrgaki = small tower) that were built in the island's suburbs in response to the surprise pirate raids. They are two-floored, square buildings of a defensive nature. Three survive today, one at Gourna, the best preserved at Lakki and another at Vayia near Ayios Theologos, with ornate designs on their collapsed walls. Intriguingly, ramparts were to remain as an architectural design feature on the roofs of a number of later buildings, primarily on the balconies, although they have now emerged as a design feature of doubtful aesthetic value on contemporary buildings, in particular in the country areas.

With the Turkish conquest, Kastro emerged as the island's leading core settlement, gradually spilling out in all directions and following the lay of the land, between the two ports of Ayia Marina and Panteli. Today, as it clambers along the slopes of the mountains, the Kastro provides a wonderful sight for the bathers at Alinda opposite, a panoramic view like an open oyster, with the castle as its shell.

The impressive economic and social development of the Lerian community in Egypt mainly, but also in Russia and Constantinople, left its seal on the island's urban development, transforming the old village into a small market town with urban characteristics. Thus, in among the small white popular houses that, tightly packed together, fought the conditions of the weather, came the large properties, the neo-classical mansions and the large town houses that, slowly, slowly, as though these too were jealous, became taller and decorated with neo-classical elements.

The island's neo-classical houses are to be found mainly at Ayia Marina. Rectangular, multi-coloured, most a shade of ochre, with tall ceilings, many with paintings and full of windows, they sing the praises of both the interior and exterior layout of the space. On entering the front door, you find yourselves in a long corridor. Spacious rooms lie to the left and to the right. Further on a wooden staircase leads to the next floor. The beautiful balconies with their iron railings are a particularly impressive feature of the neo-classical houses. In the popular houses they were made of wood, whilst here they are primarily in marble.

One particular characteristic of the island architecture are the roofs of the old houses, covered with patelia and the mantomata borders in the doors and the windows. Patelia is a purplish

mud with a clay composition that not only seals the roofs but makes them blend with the colours of the evening. As seen from the castle, this gives the island a hue that cannot be found anywhere else in the world.

One typical style of rural house found scattered throughout the island and in the hamlets is the katoikia. The ground floor is long and narrow in shape, and with the added extension forms an "L". There is a yard along its facade and length, which is covered by vines and bordered by whitewashed, stone walls known as goumoules. The windows are on the outside, with internal panels so that when the strong north winds blow the house can be lit without the windowpanes flapping. The roof is built with horizontal wooden beams known as traves, with which they even used to measure the house: instead of giving its dimensions in square metres they would say it was so many traves.

The occupation of the island by the Italians in 1912 marked the beginning of a period that was to last for 30 years, a period of architectural and town planning revolution, in particular after the Treaty of Lausanne. Traditionally, the geology of each region defined the materials that were to be used in construction. At Leros, mud (bricks), stone (mainly limestone) and porous stone were the basic materials. The winter rains called for insulation material to be used on the roofs. Seaweed, rushes and patelia covered the reeds and wood that formed the roof. The great weight of the roof required thick walls that could also be used for insulation. The giant beams of tropical wood – probably the only building material to be imported - made large open areas possible in the mansions. The Italians brought cement, iron and brick that would change the form and functions of the buildings. Military design began to dominate on the island, the fortress works being the first such intervention.

The Italian architects attempted to incorporate into their compositions elements from the islands' historical past. Public architecture gradually began to feature elements from the Byzantine, Venetian and Islamic past. They systematically ignored neo-classicism, however, which had been the main architectural style of the private residences of the Greeks of the diaspora, because they felt that this pointed ideologically to the so-called "national centre" of Athens, one of the most important centres of neo-classicism in Europe. The Italians' greatest interventions in town planning took place in Leros, where they created, from scratch, a new town, Port Lago (Lakki). Mario Lago also indicated what was to be the architectural style of the new town, Rationalism, which was the official architectural expression of the regime's public image. At Lakki, modern architecture encountered that of the Mediterranean, with the white surfaces of the cube-like buildings, flat roofs and geometric shapes. Representative buildings of this type of architecture are the works by the architects Petracco and Bernabiti in the town's administrative centre. As Vasilis Kolonas, professor in the architecture department of the University of Thessaly, writes in his book Italian Architecture in the Dodecanese:

"The church, the theatre, the school, the hospital, the military installation and, above all, the round market with the clock tower constitute a unique architectural whole that could easily be included in an international exhibition of architecture of the 1930s, that particular path between the strict austerity of early modernism and Art Deco."

The picture of Mediterranean Rationalism is completed by the Customs House, the Post Office, the Police Station and the officers' houses, the famous palatsina.

Lakki and the town Sabaudia, 100 kilometres south of Rome, are the only two cities built exclusively in the architectural order of Mediterranean Rationalism, and which have been described by Professor Antoniades as belonging to the International Style.

At the port of Ayia Marina, Italian architecture is represented by only a few buildings that blend in harmoniously with the neo-classical ones: the Police Station (in Bauhaus design), the Customs House, today home to a local radio

station, and the empty Post Office. Leros is
a museum of architectural evolution, from
the medieval pyrgakia to the Italian
Mediterranean Rationalist buildings,
a continuous dialogue of materials and
buildings, space, people and history.

1. Pretty lane at Platanos (Avlaki).
2. The neo-classical mansion of G. Kambouris
   at Ayia Marina.

4

THE KASTRO

"The church is built on a rocky eminence, behind the town and somewhat above it. A good number of people were going in the same direction as we were, the women in black, the men with clean shirts buttoned up to the neck... Above us, the church bells had started ringing. We stopped once, halfway up, to look back at the town. The white walls of the houses had on them the bloom of dying light, a kind of incandescence. Beyond them the sea lay glimmering and still. Far out in the bay a cluster of pale red lights – lanterns of fishing boats working their circular entrapment. We went on to the top of the steps."

Pascali's Island,
Barry Unsworth

The **Kastro** – the Castle – is one of the best-preserved medieval castles and the symbol of the island. Not only because it forms a geographical point of reference but mainly because, there inside its walls, is the church of the Panayia tou Kastrou. You only need to find yourself on the island on 15 August, the feast day of the Dormition of the Virgin, and to witness the thousands of people climbing the stairs that lead to the castle, out of breath but with the excitement of a sense of obligation, in order to understand.

There are two ways to reach the Kastro. The first is by road, and offers the opportunity to marvel at Panteli from up high and to visit the restored windmills that stand on its slopes. We take the road for Panteli and, a little before reaching it, turn left taking the road that goes up the mountain. At Apityki there is a wooded height near the windmills where the Lago battery installations still stand, with the barracks, the lookout and the cannon bases. The landscape below takes your breath away, with the small cape

where the German commandos disembarked literally beneath the noses of the Italian gunners during the Battle of Leros.

The second way requires patience, as you have to climb the 500 steps that lead to the peak. The steps begin at Platanos Square and provide the opportunity for you to stroll through the narrow lanes of this traditional hamlet. In amongst everything else is the abandoned building of the former Old People's Home. Beyond the **church of Ayia Paraskevi** - an impressive cruciform basilica built in 1892, which had previously been the **metropolitan church** – there are no more houses, only the remains of the old Turkish quarter with the lodgings of the kaymakam, the old Turkish governor. From here the port of Ayia Marina and the gulf of Alinda unravel beneath our feet. At the end of the route, to the left on the edge of the rock, is the small church of the **Prophet Elias**, whilst the stairs to the right lead to the central gate of the Kastro.

The Kastro of Leros is made up of three surround walls. The blocks have their own history and endurance imprinted upon them and, along with the rich but fragmentary memories of the written documents, they unravel the ball of wool of time as it rolls downwards, as the castle grows in size. The first, inner, surround wall must belong to the Byzantine era, as we can see from its manner of construction but also through the reference made to it in the bulls of 1087 and 1089, with which the castle was granted to the Blessed Christodoulos. According to the archaeologist Benson, finds from excavations here indicate that there was an ancient acropolis or citadel at this point. In 1306 the Knights of St John took over the island. The crest of Querini (1436-1453) in the wall and the testimony that in 1444, on the proposal of Querini, the Great Magister Lastic gave the order to fortify the island provide evidence that the first surround wall was repaired the latest by 1453, the year of Querini's death.

The second surround wall must have been built between 1453, when Querini died, and 1492, when it was decided to fortify the island better in order to modify it to incorporate battery fortifications. The crest dating to 1509-1511 in the third surround wall leaves no doubt as to when this wall was constructed, a process that theoretically could have lasted until 1522, when the Ottomans captured the castle. This third surround wall was designed with cannon weaponry in mind, and oral tradition comes to reinforce, albeit hesitantly, historical evidence. In 1505 the Turkish Admiral Kemal Reis, believing that the castle lacked defenders, reached Leros. Paolo Simeoni, governor of the castle, dressed local residents up in the costume of the knights and packed them into the embrasures. Kemal abandoned the siege and returned to Constantinople. The steps of the visitor, however, follow a path counter to that of time, against historical evolution. In front of the central gate, which is protected by a bastion, there is a shell that fell from a German bomber in 1943 during the battle of Leros, and which destroyed the heavy wooden door and metal plating. The semi-circular dome that covered the passageway behind the door as far as the stairwell collapsed as well. The traces of the base of the dome can still be seen today, embellished with the Mediterranean vegetation that invades the rock.

In front of us, between the third and the second surround walls, stretches out a great area dominated by the church of the Panayia tou Kastrou, the Virgin of the Castle. A map by Coronelli dating to 1688 shows that there were other buildings in this area, as well as the various "houses", the remains of which still survive, next to the north wall destroyed by the shells of the Venetian Leonardo Foscolo.

The entrance to the second surround wall was probably closed, as were many of the region's castles in this era, by a wooden drawbridge and a two-leaf heavy wooden door secured with a wooden bar. The entrance leads to a domed stoa with two cauldrons for pouring scalding water at the top. To the left of this stoa there is a peaked chapel that leads to a larger, also domed peaked church. This was the church of Ayios Georgios (Saint George), which was converted by the Knights into a Catholic church, and for this reason was known as the "Frankoklisia" (Frankish church). When the two churches united with the wall, the door in the west was closed off and turned into a cannon hole. In the niche of the offertory in the north wall there is a marble peristyle icon screen from an early Christian church.

Beneath the floor of the church there is a large well 8.5 metres deep. Inside the well bears the Amboise coat of arms.

In the depths of the stoa there is a third church, the Ayia Triada (Holy Trinity). Two crests of arms, of Querini and of Amboise, which had been moved from the outside of the well, were found in the position of the altar. The wall paintings are recent and unrelated to the history of the churches.

The Panayia tou Kastrou

"Oh, Panayia of our Kastro,
where are you in your cell
look upon my love
just as like your only child."
                                    Popular couplet

The miracle-working icon of the Panayia, the Virgin, dressed in silver and bearing the date 718 is thought to be a work of St Luke. According to a tradition recorded by T. Moschonas, "during the iconoclast era in the 9th century a small box was seen just off Leros and, within two lamps, was placed an icon of the Panayia." Clergy and commoners piously brought the icon into the Metropolitan church, where it remained until the era of the Knights. Yet, although they would transfer it to the Metropolitan church, for several days the Knights would find it the next day within the castle. They then permitted the church of the Panayia to be built within the castle. A similar tradition places the events several centuries later, when the castle was ruled by the Turks. Again, a boat would appear in the sea, with two candles and an icon. The guards informed the kaymakam and then transferred it to the Metropolitan church. The next morning the icon was found in the gunpowder store, on top of a barrel of gunpowder and with two candles in front of it. The same thing happened the next morning. The kaymakam decided that the icon should stay there. All the legends have the Panayia as mistress of the Kastro, and since the Kyra was enthroned as mistress in her castle, a white sea wish like the crown on the rocky kingdom.

The church already appears on Coronelli's 1688 map, although it is not known precisely when it was built. When the dangers posed by pirate raids died down at the end of the 17th century, the residents abandoned the castle. By 1726 no one lived there anymore, aside from around 20 pupils of Damskinos. In 1719 the newly decorated church was consecrated,

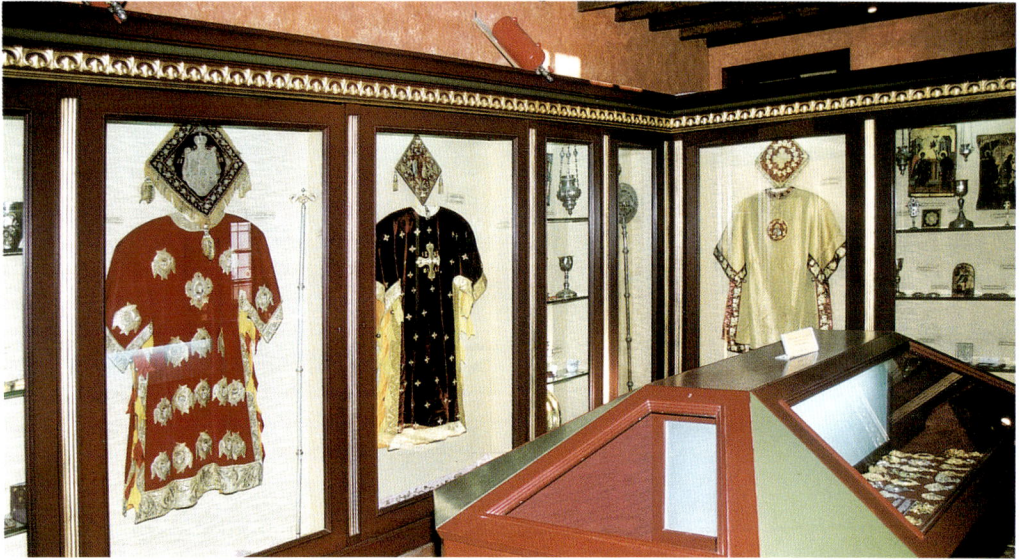

and in 1765 the cell next to the church was built, as can be seen from the inscription in the lintel of the door, perhaps by the Mount Athos monk Gregory, who had returned to Leros. In a codex dating to 1765 a large number of gifts to the Panayia are recorded, which were later used in maintaining the Greek schools.

On the east side of the church there was a building that was recently redecorated and which operates as the Museum of the Metropolitan Church. The exhibits include Byzantine icons, holy vessels, vestments and valuable objects that were transferred there from the whole of the island. There is also the old, invaluable library of the Panayia tou Kastrou and a few archaeological finds. In 1892, with financial support provided by Anneta Iatroudaki, the paved stoa with the stone terrace bordering onto the church was built. In 1973 the pebbles were placed in the joints of the paving, creating the two designs. The church is built with large grey blocks that were perhaps taken from the ruins of houses and other buildings on the Kastro. On the east side, and primarily in the semi-hexagonal apse, relief sculpture has been carved into the stone. Above the main east entrance there is a marble signed epistyle, which is perhaps the continuation of a similar one found in the church of the Ayia Triada.

Inside the church, which was recently paved with irregular tiles, the wooden icon stand, set up with the financial support of two Lerians in 1745, is in a Baroque style. The gold inlay was completed 40 years later. From the original silver inlay that was to be used on another icon, only to be replaced in 1762 by gold and silver, the Panayia's halo and a section that covered Christ's right side have been removed. Three semi-precious stones have also been removed from Christ's halo. From the initial twelve Russian icons of the Dodekaorton (the twelve disciples) at the top of the icon stand only six remain and the remainder have been replaced with contemporary icons. The wood-carved pulpit and Bishop's throne were created in the 19th century, most likely by a workshop from the island of Symi.

There are two other important icons. One large icon from the middle of the 18th century, with Ayios Gerasimos and Ayios Georgios, perhaps a gift from the Lerian Bishop of Herakleia, Gerasimos, is today housed in the museum. An icon dedicated to Methodius, another Lerian Bishop of Herakleia, entered the church in 1783. This is an icon of the Theotokos Vrefokratousa ("the Mother of God holding the Infant") with the eponym Hodegitria (Guide), the whole of the lower part of which is inlaid in gold, within a special frame that bears an inscription. In the south, the church is linked to a cell dating to 1765, as can be seen by the date on the lintel. The cell houses a small exhibition of ecclesiastical items. The large icons of Christ Pantocrater, Panayia Glykofilousa and St John the Evangelist in the icon stand date to the 16th century and are works of the famed Cretan school of painting, essentially the last great period of Byzantine art, at a time when Byzantium no longer existed. The other two large icons on the icon stand, those of Ayios Nikolaos and John the Baptist, date to after the 18th century.

In addition to forming a unique conversation with history and the overpowering presence of the Panayia in the behaviour and attitudes of the Greeks, a visit to the castle provides an outburst of aesthetics. The rock, the blue of the sky and the turquoise of the sea. The whole of the green journey, from the colour of the leaves to the deep shades of the cypress tree and the night-time that ascends from the sea, stealing the purple from the roofs. And later, black velvet with the pins of the stars and the lights that tremble beside and within the sea.

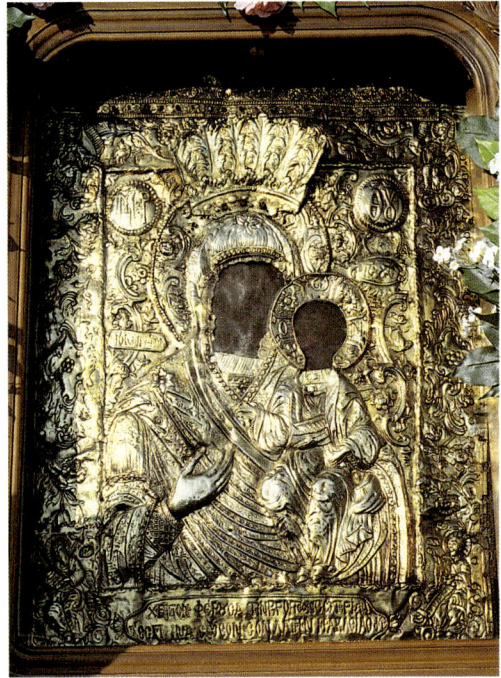

1. Room in the Kastro Museum.
2, 3. Icon and icon stand from the church of the Panayia tou Kastrou.

5

LAKKI

"Most of the works by the architects Petracco and Bernabiti are included among the works considered as representative examples of this architecture in the Dodecanese. The most important among them are the buildings of the administrative centre at Lakki, which is literally a museum of modern architecture in the Greek context, an identification, finally, of the modern with the Aegean."

Italian Architecture in the Dodecanese,
Vasilis Kolonas

Late in the evening the boat reaches the natural harbour of Lakki, the largest in the south-east Mediterranean. The town suddenly appears in front of the eyes of the visitor, as the opening of the gulf, only 400 metres, hides it quite well… Closed all around by mountains, Lakki is like a port. Porto Lago, the Port-Lake, the Italians called it, and not by chance. The Italians closed the entrance and thus blocked the allied ships with an underwater net, the remains of which can still be seen at Katsouni.

Before the take-over of the island by the Italians, Lakki was nothing more than a rural suburb, with a few houses full of stagnant water. The neo-classical house of the Roussos family still stands on the peak of the hill and next to the remains of Yiannis Plitzounia's windmill. Descending from behind the Elementary School, hidden in amongst the trees, a medieval pyrgaki still stands the tests of time, although without its roof. Above the mantomata of the only entrance there is a pointed Arab arch and, higher up, the spot for the cauldron of boiling water or oil, which the inhabitants would pour onto the pirates who attempted to break through the door. Its toothed ramparts stand complete.

Panoramic view of the gulf of Lakki.

Plan of Lakki

1. Roma Hotel (Albergo Roma)
2. Roma Cinema and Theatre
   (Cinema e teatro Roma)
3. Market (Mercato)
4. Residential and commercial zone
   (Zone residenziali e commerciali)
5. Customs House (Dogana)
6. Elementary School
   (Scuola elementare e asilo)
7. Italian Town Hall (Municipio e casa
   del fascio)
8. Workers' residences (Case per operai)
9. Officers' residences (Case per ufficiali)
10. Non-commissioned Officers' residences
    (Case INCIS)
11. Infantry barracks (Caserma Regina)
12. Naval barracks (Caserma dei marinai)
13. Church of St Francis (Chiesa di San Francesco)
    – Ayios Nikolaos
14. Scouts (Casa del Balilla) – no longer standing

Platanos, the Kastro, Panteli and Pitiki.

On the other edge of the port at Gonia stands the mansion of Antonellos, with its arches, where the Italians set up their first Nautical Centre (today it belongs to the Leros Naval Technical Installations Service, or YNTEL) and a little further up, on the road up to Koulouki, is the neo-classical villa of Odysseus Bellenis (today the director's residence). This is where the Italian Admiral Mascherpa stayed. A little above, towards the hospital, is the two-floored neo-classical house of Matantos, which today houses the Port Authority.

The Italians chose this natural harbour, peaceful like a lake, to install their large aeronautical base, thus competing for the control of the east Mediterranean. In 1923 the aeronautical base Gianni Rossetti, which took its name from the first pilot who was killed, was built at Lepida, in an area that belonged to the diaspora Greek from Egypt Nikolaos Tsigadas-Pashas. Tsigadas's villa, standing in the middle of a well-designed garden, hosted the Officers' Club. There were continuous alterations between 1927 and 1932, which finally ensured the necessary extension for the creation of a base that was divided into a south-west zone, with military and technical installations, and a residential zone in the north-east. The first included hangars for hydroplanes, storerooms, offices, the administration centre and the hostel for the pilots. The residential zone included one- and two-storey houses. The housing needs of the officers and their families were constantly increasing, however, and they led the Italian authorities to the decision to found a new town on the opposite coast. In 1934 the town plan for Porto Lago was approved, most likely the work of Rodolfo Petracco, and by 1936 it had 7,500 inhabitants. In addition to the military installations, it included everything necessary for a town: administrative, cultural and social services, as well as distinct residential zones for the officers (single and double dwellings), non-commissioned officers (two-storey complexes with four dwellings) and workers (two-storey apartment buildings).

The town plan, in a butterfly design, which is a unique example of the International Style (see Architecture), is built around the logic of a large, central avenue along the waterfront. This is intersected by a perpendicular axial route that leads to a second, inner square and ending at a small hill, where a statue or some other kind of monument would have confirmed the fascist dominance.

Giant works were carried out in order to dry out the large swamps, whilst eucalyptus trees were also planted. A particular technique was used for the foundations of the building complexes. They would pin large tree trunks to the wet earth, nail iron beams onto them, and then pave the floor and pour concrete over it.

The tour of the town can start from its edge, at the Elementary School (scuola elementare) which also housed the nursery (asilo) and was run by the nuns. Construction of the building started in 1934 and was completed in 1936 according to designs by R. Petracco. On the first floor there is a small chapel dedicated to the Virgin, with the typical characteristics of Catholic churches. The arched colonnade in the south side makes it stand out from afar, whilst its interior, with the atrium, is impressive. Next to the school was the Customs House (Regio Dogana di Porto Lago), with the characteristic crest on the wall. Today it houses the Officers' Club. The building was begun in 1933 and it has had tacky minor renovations that can easily be replaced.

The coastal road (la passegiata sul mare), which still has the typical Italian small columns with the pipes, is dominated by the Albergo Roma hotel, adjacent to the cinema and theatre building (cinema e teatro Roma). These were both built by the engineer Sardeli, probably according to the designs of A. Bernabiti in the years 1936-1938. The cinema and theatre, originally called Puccini, had a removable roof that no longer exists today. It hosted performances by primarily amateur troupes. The hotel building was distorted in 1955 when the balcony railings were removed and replaced by continuous balconies on the south and west sides. Small balconies with railings survive at the back of the building.

Opposite the other edge of the small open square stands the Italian Town Hall of Lakki (Municipio di Porto Lago), a work of A. Bernabiti (1935-1938). The building housed the Italian Town Hall on the first floor, the revenue service, the Fascio (the fascist organisation offices), the youth club, the meeting rooms of the Black Shirts, a games room known as the Dopo Lavoro. On the ground floor were the Post Office (Posta) and the Italian pharmacy. The fascist guard (Milizia) was installed in an extension of the building in 1936.

After the bombardments destroyed a section of the building (where the cafeteria is today), tacky interventions were made, such as the balconies and aluminium that have distorted the aesthetic of the building to a great degree, although the remainder retains its original form.

Continuing across the length of the coastal avenue we reach the modern building that houses the Leros High School, a building that looks very similar to the design drawn by A. Bernabiti for the Italian High School that was never built. A perpendicular road leads to the island's old people's home, housed in the buildings of the old Italian hospital. Next to the naval installations is the women's section of the psychiatric hospital.

On the coast in front of the High School there is a monument with the names of the victims of the Queen Olga, and the bust of the ship's captain, G. Blessa.

On the morning of 26th September 1943, the feast day of Ayios Theologos and a Sunday, the Queen Olga had just docked at the port of Lakki after going out on patrol, and it was moored next to the British destroyer the HMS Intrepid. Suddenly, the two ships were attacked by 62 German Ju-88 planes, and at 10.11 the Greek destroyer was sunk, split in two. The captain, five officers, ten non-commissioned officers and 54 sailors were lost. A little later the Intrepid, which was towed into the shallow waters, came under a new air attack and was sunk completely.

Next to the High School is the impressive building of the naval barracks (Caserma dei Marinai), built in 1929 on the design of R. Petracco, bearing the freedom of form possible before De Vecchi imposed Rationalism. It is a combination of arabesque and north Italian eclecticism, and differs from the Rationalist style of the other buildings in Lakki. Next to this is a large warehouse built in 1933.

Behind the Hotel Roma, the market building (Mercato di Portolago) can be seen from afar, with the atrium and the clock built according to designs by Petracco and which began to be constructed in 1934, being completed in 1936.

The impressive building of the naval barracks.

On the first floor of this building were the Italian High School and the internal structures of the clocks, and services provided by the Italian local government. The building won an award at the Italian Rationalism exhibition during the Venice Biennial of 1976.

A little further up, next to the public spring beneath the trees, we encounter the bust of a skinny man. This is Emanuel Gedeon, academic, medievalist and historian of the years after the Fall of Constantinople. A Megas Chartophylax (a metropolitan ecclesiastical official with judicial responsibilities) of the Patriarchate of Constantinople and Ypomnimatografos (Commentarius) of the Church of Jerusalem, Gedeon was born in Constantinople to Lerian parents in 1851 and died in Athens in 1943. In 1981 his bones were transferred to Leros. A section of his personal archives can be found in the General State Archives – Regional Archive of Leros at Platanos.

Continuing from the small coastal square along the central perpendicular road with the residences of the Italian officers (palazzina), we reach the circular square of Paris Roussos. His bust stands in the centre of the square, with a pebbled circular surface.

Paris Roussos was the scion of a well-known shipping family. He contributed his wealth to the struggle for the liberation of the Dodecanese and to incorporate them in the rest of Greece. He took part as a representative of the Dodecanese Union in the Paris Conference at the close of World War One. Using his own funds he published, in London in January 1919, Skevos Zervos's book The Dodecanese, in English, French and Greek.

At the edge of Roussos Square stands the magnificent building of the Caserma Regina, which

housed the Italian 10th Infantry regiment. This was built in 1934 on designs by Petracco with fascist elements in its facade. Today it houses the PIKPA psychiatric hospital.

Between the central road that leads to Platanos and the building with the cinema and theatre stretches out a zone with combined residential and commercial activities (zone residenziali e commerciali). The buildings tend to have shops on the ground floor and workers' apartments on the first floor. It is worth having a look at the street with the small shops (via magazzino), in a semi-circular arrangement, with the typical coverings. Continuing along the central road after the church of Ayios Nikolaos the Case INCIS spreads out. This is a complex of six different residences, two to the left and four to the right, with apartments in each one, which were occupied mainly by officers.

The church of Ayios Nikolaos emerged from the catholic church of St Francis with the addition of a vestibule. The Church of St Francis (chiesa di San Francesco) was built between the years 1935-1939, by the engineer Sardeli on the designs, most likely, of A. Bernabiti. The church was bombed in 1943 and repaired using cement blocks.

Today Lakki still has its large tree-lined avenues. In addition to the many commercial shops and bars and cafes along the waterfront, there is a marina and a boat filling station.

1. The monument to Paris Roussos in the square of the same name.
2. The Holy Monastery of Ayios Theologos (11th c. AD).
3. The Roma Cinema and Theatre.
4. Ayios Nikolaos.
5. The market building, with the Clock Tower.

6

The tour of the island is relatively easy, as the old Italian roads, all surfaced today, cover almost the whole of the island. There is a central surfaced axial road, lined with eucalyptus trees, which are, unfortunately, being constantly destroyed, and which connects the whole island. Many side roads start from this central road, some with an asphalt surface, others simply dirt tracks in an otherwise good condition, leading to all the corners of the island. The fortress structures of the island, which functioned as a great aeronautical base, presupposed the existence of a dense road network that connected the coastal batteries with defence points on the perimeter. A leftover from that era is the island's great road network as well as an open-air military history museum of the First World War.

For the tour of the island, which can be done without long stops and in one day, in addition to a car, there are many taxis and a bus with two to three daily connections.

1st Route
Lakki – Temenia - Xerokampos (p. 69)

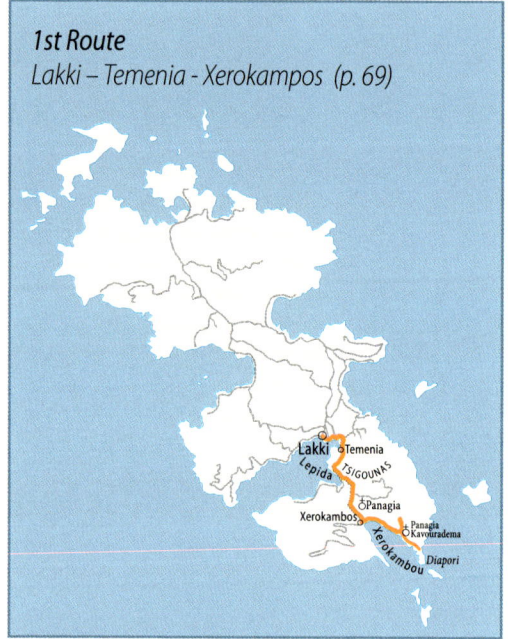

2nd Route
Lakki – Koulouki – Merikia – Katsouni (p. 72)

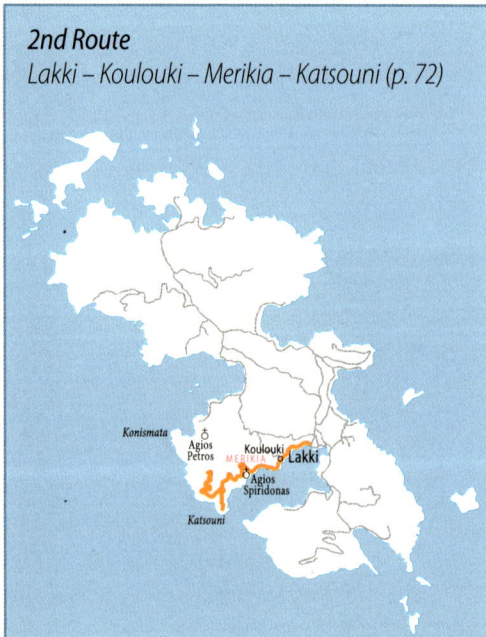

3rd Route
Lakki – Vromolithos – Panteli – Platanos (p. 76)

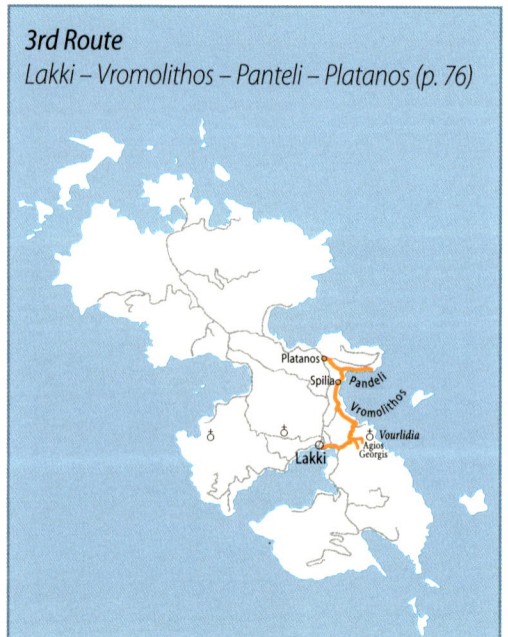

TOUR OF THE ISLAND

4th Route
Ayia Marina – Krithoni - Alinda (p. 86)

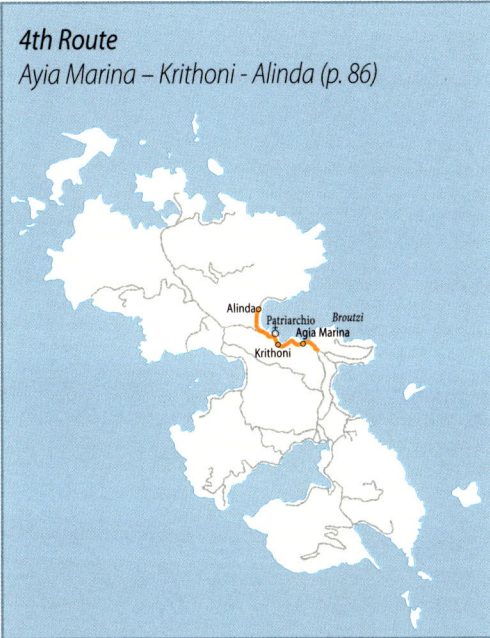

Alinda
Patriarchio   Broutzi
Agia Marina
Krithoni

5th Route
Alinda – Panayies – Dyo Diskaria (p. 97)

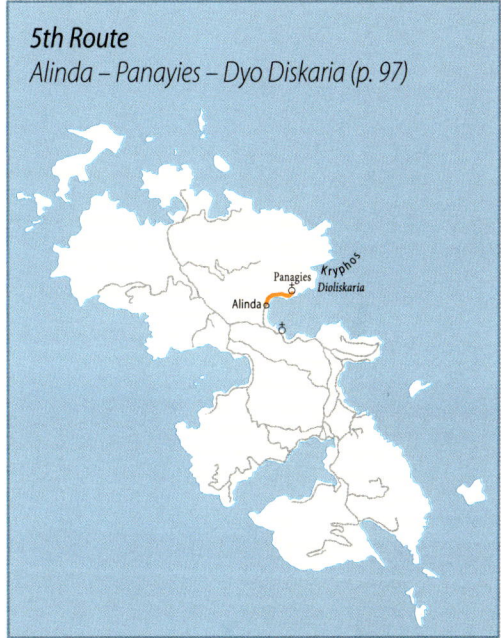

Panagies   *Kryphos*
Dioliskaria
Alinda

6th Route
Alinda – Gourna - Drymonas – Ayios Theologos (p. 102)

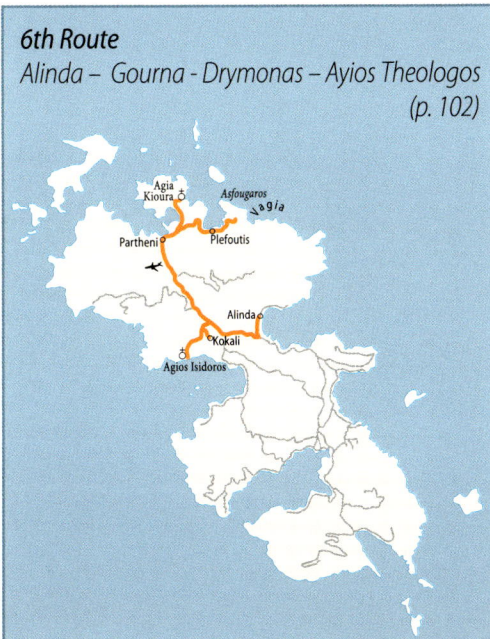

Agia
Kioura   *Asfougaros*
Vagia
Partheni   Plefoutis
Alinda
Kokali
Agios Isidoros

7th Route
Alinda – Ayios Isidoros – Partheni – Plefoutis (p.108)

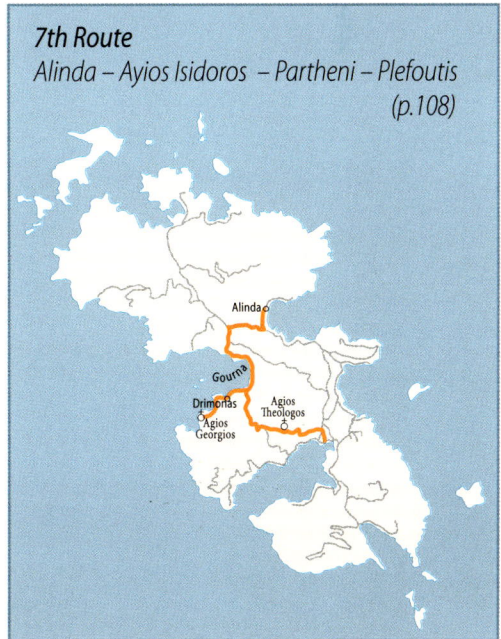

Alinda
Gourna
Drimonas   Agios
Theologos
Agios
Georgios

1

2

Lakki - Temenia - Xerokampos

Leaving Lakki and the small, artificial cape with a small grove on the hill behind, following the coastal road, we reach the old suburb of Temenia, which is immortalised in a Byzantine imperial bull of the 11th century. Past the factory of the Italian electricity company SIER (1936), which today houses the DEH (Greek electricity board) and whatever has survived of the carbonated drinks producer Doliani, we encounter the small church o the Ayioi Anargyroi. This church is described in the aforementioned bull as the "church of the Ayioi Anargyroi, domed, with a long narrow plan, furnished with doors, painted and with gold-leafed icons." An inscription on the door lintel indicates that the form the church has today must date to 1907.

To the left of the church a small road leads to the Italian cemetery (cimitero cattolico), built in 1936 on the designs most likely of Petracco. The entrance is preserved in its original form, with the iron cross at the peak. The cemetery is today used by locals, whilst the Italian burials on the left are reminders of the past. There is a poignancy to the area with the small crosses and sparse burials, final resting places of the patients of the psychiatric hospital.

After Temenia, on the approach to the Psychiatric hospital, one can make out, on the opposite side of the small cape, the crane that transferred the hydroplanes to the sea and the base of the hangar carved into the mountain. Next to the administration centre of the G. Rossetti aeronautical base, and a little further down, are the residences of the base's pilots with the large assembly area in front of them. Today these buildings, as with all the buildings of the base at Lepida, belong to the Leros State Infirmary.

In 1923, after the signing of the Treaty of Lausanne and the final hand over of the islands to the Italians, they selected the area where the Tsigada-Pasha villa stood at **Lepida**, drenched in greenery, to set up an aeronautical base. Once we have passed through the entrance, which has preserved its characteristic Italian architecture,

1. Tsigadas Pashas's villa at Temenia.
2. Temenia.
3. The church of the Ayioi Anargyroi at Temenia.

we find ourselves in the officers' residential area of the base. Continuing the road past the crane, we reach the area of **Ayios Georgis**, which today belongs to the YNTEL. When the Italians began to set up the base, they knocked down the church that was here. The icon of Saint George was taken by Madam Antonelou, who later married an Italian. The many accidents that took place forced the governor to build a small shrine to place the icon. The submarine station was installed at Ayios Georgios, with workshops, cisterns, a naval repairs unit and a floating cistern. The large buildings were built in 1936, which housed the submarine crews and the other military personnel. In 1949 these buildings became home to the Royal Technical Schools, better known as the Schools of Frederica (after the Queen of Greece), in which children from all over Greece were housed. When a strong wind cracked the shrine a few days before King Paul died, Frankoulis, the Director of the Schools, had the small church of Ayios Georgios that stands today built. The schools were closed in 1964, and in 1967 they were converted by the military junta that had taken over Greece into a concentration camp for political prisoners. They were later used to hold the "heavy cases" of the Psychiatric Hospital, better known from the newspapers as "Kiosk 19". Today the building is full of historical memories, and stands on the point of collapse.

A detour after the Psychiatric Hospital leads to Tsingouna and the refuse dump next to the quarry. For those interested, the otherwise unpleasant route reveals two Italian billets of the 113th Battery as well as a panoramic view of Lakki and a different aspect of Panteli for photography.

The central road continues as far as **Xerokampos**. At the entrance to the village an inclining road to the left leads to Paliokastro. A well-preserved Italian lookout point on the road, another in the yard of a house and the wall of a storeroom come like scenes from a war in the peaceful atmosphere of the village, reminders that the area was once a military zone. The traces of Cyclopean walls indicate the possible presence of an ancient acropolis. There was also an ancient signalling station here, which according to Oikonomopoulos (1888) was used as a lighthouse. Today there is a small church of the Panayia, which celebrates its feast day on 15 August, with a service held partially outside, giving a panoramic view of Xerokampos. On the site of the small church there was once a much larger early Christian church, of which little remains apart from traces of the narthex and of the mosaics, which some have unfortunately attempted to cement over.

At the entrance to the village, where a small verdant valley spreads out between two mountain massifs, we encounter the church of **Ayios Fanourios**, built in 1961 by workers and students at the Royal Technical Schools. Ayios Fanourios is the patron saint of the village and his feast day is held on 17 August. On this day the local residents prepare fanouropites, Fanouri pies, some of which are exceptionally tasty. These are shared out at the church among the people who have gathered here from all over the island. If we continue along the little road that passes in front of the church of Ayios Fanarios then we reach the old quarry.

A few metres further down, the small church of **Ayios Nikolaos** stands on the site of another early Christian church. The dirt road going up the slope of the mountain leads to Skoumparda,

from where the view is amazing. Of particular interest are the scattered installations of the San Giorgio battery, which gave inspiration to both the book and film of The Guns of Navarone. Indeed, on the south side juts out the steep, almost sheer slope with the pill boxes scattered almost like eagles' nests and where Anthony Quinn, David Niven and the allied commandoes scrambled up, cinematically speaking of course.

On the return journey we come again to the central road that leads to the quiet fishing port of Xerokampos, a popular mooring place for yachts and with fish tavernas serving fresh fish. A small caique boat departs every morning for Xerokampos from Kalymnos, returning in the early afternoon. The surfaced road continues as far as **Panayia tin Kavouradaina**, a small church built among the rocks and next to the sea, which can be reached via the steps that that begin at the road. According to tradition the icon of the Panayia was found in a crack in the rock inside the sea. After Panayia tin Kavouradaina the road becomes a dirt track again, reaching as far as Diapori. Above the road

you can see, hidden behind the trees, the Italian katzarma, Battery 388. The word katzarma is the local Greek version of the Italian "case di armi" (barracks). It is worth clambering up to this point. The serenity of the landscape together with the wall paintings, designed by some unknown Italian artist, transport you back in time. The remains of the bombarded Battery 281 stand at Diapori, whilst right opposite, at a little distance, are the Glaronisia and Kalymnos. Legend tells that a Kalymnian shepherd, Alachouzos, swam across every day, going from one of the Glaronisia to another, putting his clothes into a goatskin, in order to reach his beloved at Xerokampos.

1. The little church of the Panayia at Xerokampos.
2. The church of Ayios Fanourios.
3. The Panayia Kavouradaina.
4. Panoramic view of Xerokampos.

4

Lakki - Koulouki - Merikia - Katsouni

One route, particularly ideal for walking within the greenery as far as Merikia, begins above the port jetty and the abandoned Italian jail at the port near the anti-aircraft battery. This small wood, flowing with eucalyptus trees, cypresses and pines, was used by the Italians as camouflage for their military installations. The wood previously grew unimpeded, as livestock rearing was kept far from these enclosed zones, in contrast to today, when goats graze freely, thus preventing its further extension. It is characteristic that you can spot the Italian katzarmes among the wooded cover surrounding them.

The journey follows the coastline, and from the side of the road you can see the entrances to the underground stoas, where the ammunitions were stored, as this side of the gulf was home to both the open-air and the underground materials and ammunitions storerooms. The route kicks off at two picturesque gulfs known as the **Kouloukia**. In the first gulf an old, outdoor restaurant right next to the waves pops out suddenly from among the trees, as though in a scene from an old Greek movie of the 1960s. The restored Italian storeroom in the next gulf is today home to the island's Yachting Circle.

The asphalt road ends at **Merikia** beach, behind which sections of the large Italian storerooms pop out, as though in a giant set design. The abandoned headquarters of the unit stand at the edge of the gulf, whilst in the same direction, behind the trees, there commences a series of semi-outdoor storerooms in the shape of small mounds. The series ends at the small Byzantine church of **Ayios Zacharias**, which is literally built into the remains of another, larger one. Behind Ayios Zacharos are the bombarded installations, one could say Italian slaughterhouses. Another route starts from here, among the trees that run alongside the Sykamia gorge and finally reach the island's central, small mountain range.

The road after Merikia is a dirt road, passing **Kokkina**, a small, pretty beach with a smugglers' boat at the edge. Behind the beach are the abandoned installations of the old pig farm, with the church of Ayios Spyridon at the bottom of the stream and an Italian katzarma above this. The dirt road continues past Porcelania, an area famed for its mud (porcelain) and also a place of execution for the Germans. On this route, as on all the island's old Italian roads, it is worth looking out for the small Italian stone bridges built over the streams.

On reaching the area of Katsounia we are welcomed, on behalf of the memory of the era, by two columns (one collapsed) at the entrance to the military base. One road leads to the edge of the gulf, where the billets were, and the site of the engine that tugged the anti-submarine net, with the column that wound the cables. The bases of the 250th Gunnery and the 227th Battery can also be seen. Returning to the central road, we reach the installations of the Ducci battery, where there are a well and gunnery bases. A not particularly pleasant road leads to the Patella rise. This was where the headquarters of the FAM DI CAT were, in other words the headquarters for the coordination of all the anti-aircraft system. It had facilities for locating aeroplanes, of which the cement base of one still survives. The billets can also be seen, as can an observation post and the base of an anti-aircraft machine gun.

The dirt road continues above the small cape of Konismata, which can be reached on foot. Taking a twist and a turn, it arrives at the Monastery of the Panayia in the centre of the island. A fork in the road after Thermokipia leads to Ayios Petros and then to Panayia Gourlomata, before reaching the region of Drymonas. The other branch leads past some cattle farms before reaching Fytoia, from there returning to Lakki via a slip road.

1. The little byzantine church of Ayios Zacharias.
2. The church of Ayios Petros.
3. View of the second Koulouki, with the Yachting Circle.
4. The picturesque beach of Kokkino..

3RD ROUTE

Lakki - Vromolithos - Panteli - Platanos

The central road from Lakki leads to Platanos, which has almost merged into it. Three large antennas can be seen on the left of the road, where a turning leads to the district of Ayios Nikolaos. Many of the buildings of the Italian radio transmitter still stand here, with their secured windows and other remnants.

The central road at this point ascends amongst laurel leaves. Eucalyptus trees appear again at the turn where three branches fork off on the right and another to the left.

The road that turns to the left ascends and crosses through this lush green side of the island that is protected from the north winds. We leave Myloi on the left behind us and reach **Rachi**, perched on a spot in the centre of the island with a panoramic view. The view from here is stunning, and stretches out over the gulfs of Ayia Marina and Gourna. In business lingo, it is the most strategic location on the island. This is perhaps why ferocious battles took place here in November of '43, for the takeover of the island. Here, in a crazy campaign, German parachutists descended, suffering great losses.

A dirt road leads to Merovigli, but access is forbidden. The road then leads down and reaches Alinda.

The first branch to the right leads to the height of **Vigla**, where the 306th Battery was. This is one of the most impressive fortress positions on the island, with entrance tunnels in the positions of the gunners and the billet.

The second branch leads to **Tourkopigado**, a beautiful verdant slope that leads to small ports and continues as far as the little church of Ayios Georgios at Vourlida, in a completely deserted beach.

The third branch to the right goes down to the beach of **Vromolithos**, one of the island's most beautiful leeward beaches with vegetation growth reaching as far as the waves and the picturesque little rocks at the edge. Unfortunately, it is also a beloved place of anchorage for yachts in the summer. Opposite stands the islet of Ayia Kyriaki, with the church of the same name. Vromolithos is the most ideal spot on the island for passing nights with a full moon, which springs out suddenly from the sea giving magical dimensions to the night sky. At a site where only a few years ago there stood only a neo-classical villa and one or two houses, today it is packed with rented rooms.

1. The Mills.
2. Panoramic view of Vromolithos.

Continuing, the road leads out again onto the central road at **Spilia**, a densely-built neighbourhood with almost rectangular, two-storey houses. The rocky land here has left little room for free space. The road narrows markedly here and the houses literally stand on the street. Traffic is unbelievable in the summer, when the population almost doubles. The renowned spring of Kalikaris also stands here – tradition holds that any visitor who drinks water from it will fall in love and stay on the island for ever. Kalikaris was a cobbler, and he thus took his name from his profession (a kaliki was a shoe with an iron tip). The first neo-classical and town houses begin to appear, giving an atmosphere of bygone days. The castle with the hamlet of Platanos spreading out over the slopes beneath it and in between the impressive, large parish churches of Ayia Paraskevi and the Metamorphosis of Christ can be spotted in the spaces between the houses. Both churches were built in 1892, Ayia Paraskevi in a cruciform basilica style with money from the Lerian community of Cairo, and the Metamorphosis of Christ in a domed basilica style with money from the community of Alexandria. The "competition" as to which would be bigger and the lack of space made both churches particularly grand, dominating the fringes of the hamlet.

The road turns right for **Panteli** a little before it reaches the square of Platanos. Although Panteli has now merged in to Platanos, it still preserves its autonomy and the atmosphere of a small fishing village. Narrow roads, white houses, nets spread out over the pavements, yards with geraniums, fishing boats and the tables of the fish tavernas flirting with the waves next to the sea. The aromas of salt, iodine, paint and fried fish all blend sweetly together. If you are lucky, some enthusiast might start playing his tsabouna bagpipes.

Returning to the central road, we reach the small square of Platanos, the heart of the island.

Views of Panteli.

Platanos

*"I have a love at Christos
and a love on the castle
and a love up at Platanos
that reigns over the stars"*

Havas of Loulourgas

The long and narrow square is positioned between two mountain massifs, and took its name from an old platanos (plane tree) that stood here in 1765. There are two plane trees in the square, one on the castle side on the edge of the square and the other in front of the Town Hall.

The section of the town beneath the Kastro, which reached as far as Platanos and united it with Ayia Marina and Panteli, used to be known as Horio. The houses beneath the castle are small, poor and densely built, with steep, narrow roads that get lost among the yards. Ayia Paraskevi, the old metropolitan church, used to form the centre of Horio. The most central point then shifted to the old Girls School. In the lower parts were the parish church of Christ and, in the direction of Ayia Marina, the church of the Evangelistria, today's metropolitan church.

In the past the square had been stone paved, whilst next to the plane tree there was a large spring and beneath it a fountain, the water being brought here from Merovigli via an arched aqueduct. Around the square there were many cafes, the Government House, tax office and police, all located in old, little houses. Adjacent to the square was the parish church of the Cross, built in the form that still survives today from 1854, even though the marble inscription above the lintel of the entrance hints at surprises that may come to light in a future archaeological excavation. The interior of the church is an impressive example of the island order, with a wooden iconstand, women's section and a wood-carved and painted pulpit. The demogerontia would hold its meetings and votes in the churchyard.

Platanos, the Kastro and Panteli.

The plane tree in the central square of the village. Right, lanes in Platanos and, below, the churches of the Evangelismos and Ayia Paraskevi in front of the Kastro.

In 1873 the Lerian Brotherhood of Egypt was founded in Cairo, and the leading Lerians of Egypt decided to take the island's future into their own hands. Until the end of the century, Leros was an island undergoing transformation. Between Platanos, the old boundaries of Horio and the opposite slope of Merovigli, a new town filled with grand public buildings and neo-classical private houses began to run down to Ayia Marina, taking over the open space.

Today in the square, the building of the Town Hall stands out, built by Nikolaos Tsigadas-Pasha in 1900 to house the Police and Gendarmerie Station. Next to the Town Hall, with the classical pediment on its facade is the historical Lerian Club, inside of which time seems to have stood still.

On the side of the building, next to the road, a small section of the pebbled area of the square has survived. A small, upward road leads to the building of the Demogerontia, also known as the Old Town Hall. A marble plaque in the wall of the facade reads:

DEMOGERONTIA OF LEROS 1899
BUILT AT THE EXPENSE OF NIKOLAOS TSIGADAS BEY

The ground floor once housed the Community Pharmacy and the Town Clinic used to operate there. Today it is home to the Public Library, in which is kept the fine private library of Adamantios Haramis (1830-1885) that had so impressed the historian Karl Krumbacher when he visited Leros. The same building also houses the Regional Archive of Leros of the General State Archives, with valuable archive material on the island, including the original architectural designs of the Italian buildings.

Continuing up Nikoloudis Street, we encounter the church of the Cross, an old town house and the remains of a mill. Turning right, we come out into a small square with neo-classical houses dominated by the grand residence of Nikoloudis, a former government minister, which today houses the county court. The Italian insignia in the wall has remained from the days when the building belonged to the Italian administration.

The upward road continues and encounters the central peripheral road in front of Angelou's characteristic turquoise neo-classical house. The peripheral road, which starts in the region of Ankyra above Vromolithos, near the hamlet of Roubou that is decorated with bombshells from the war, bypasses the summer traffic and leads out of Ayia Marina on the road towards Alinda. The road offers a panoramic view of Kastro with the town at its foot - particularly spectacular at night when it is lit.

The old spring of Palaiaskloupi (Old Asklepios) is also on this road, next to which it is believed there once stood a sanctuary of Asklepios, the god of healing. The waters from this spring fed the aqueduct at Platanos. It is worth noting the entirely unbalanced distribution of the springs. All the springs, 11 at the end of the 19th century and five now, are found beneath Merovigli, whilst there is not a single one beneath the castle on the other side. This is, of course, natural given the geological makeup of the mountain, with the underlying porous limestone above the waterproof clay. This geology is also expressed in the vegetation, of which D. Oikonomopoulos's 1888 description is characteristic: "The mountain of Merovigli as far as the centre is bare and dry, but further down and as far as its lower feet earthy and lush in vegetation."

An explanation for the origin of the name is given by the Russian traveller Barsky, who visited the island in 1731: "A viglator (lookout) always sits at the peak of the mountain, looking out all day long for which direction the small and large boats arrive from, and with a stentorian voice announces their arrival."

A little further down, a steep side road leads to Patelos, a particular neighbourhood with small ground floors that do not face on to the small square, and other features of a refugee neighbourhood. Above this point, at Merovigli – today a military zone – the 127th Battery had been stationed. The administration centre of the island's defence along with British Commander Tinley's headquarters had been based here within a great converted cave during the Battle of Leros. And this is where

A lane leading to Ayia Paraskevi (above) and general view of Platanos and the Kastro (on the right).

the last act of the war took place, on 16 November 1943, with the cession of the British forces, packed inside the cave, which had been encircled by German troops. Tinley himself emerged from the cave and gave himself up, bearing a white flag.

We return to Platanos Square. At its edge, opposite the Town Hall, begin the stepped lanes that lead to Ayia Paraskevi and the Kastro. A road to the right leads to the neighbourhood of Christ, with the church of the Metamorphosis of the Saviour that had been completed by Tsigadas-Pasha. Before going to the church it is worth visiting the town house of Irene Kandioglou, which has preserved its old decoration intact and today operates as a museum. Of particular interest in this house is the old secret hideout, which many houses of its day had. The old pebbled yard is preserved around the church with capital letters discernable in one part, perhaps the name of the builder.

Pebbles were quite common on the roads and in the yards of old Leros. The pebbles were prepared in the traditional way. On the smooth side that was formed with well-trodden red earth they would place a thin layer of limestone to keep the pebbles in their place. In order to pave a square kilometre they would need around three cans of pebbles picked one by one from the beach. The pebbles must be flat so as not to leave cracks between them, and be around 6-9 cm long. The pebbles used for background must be white in colour and those used for decorative elements black. The square of Platanos itself is paved with pebbles, as are many old roads.

Many forgotten little roads survive today, such as that with the steps that leads from Christos to Panteli. The pebbled yard of the neo-classical town house of Madame Foka below the county court is particularly impressive, whilst a little further up in the yard of an indigo town house there are pebbles with delightful designs. There are remains of pebbled paving in the Elementary School at Ayia Marina, by the busts of Evangelos at the Bellenio High School, of Papanastasis at Ayia Marina and of Roussos at Lakki, not to mention the yard of the church of the Panayia at Kastri and in the yard of the so-called Patriarchate.

In Platanos Square, on the road going towards Christos, a little road on the left leads down towards Ayia Marina. This is a section of old Leros that is distinguished by the neo-classical mansions of Boulafentis and Antonelos standing opposite the church of the Evangelismos. The road ends in front of the Elementary School.

In addition to the Demogerontia and the Town Hall, Tsigadas-Pasha built the square of Platanos and the Municipal Market (no longer standing) as well as the Bishopric next to the church of the Evangelismos. One important work of his, which essentially unites Platanos with Ayia Marina, is the paved central road. As a decree of the day notes, "worthy of a great memory the nation-loving gentleman Nikolaos Tsigadas, patron of the Town Hall, Government House, the Public Road, and beneficiary of the church of Christ and Charitable foundations…"

Ayia Marina - Krithoni – Patriarchate

Let us walk down, then, with history and the modernising wind that reaches from the borders of Hellenism at the end of the 19th century, filling Leros with charitable foundations and neo-classical buildings. The narrow road leading downwards leaves the tiled house of Roussos on the right and passes in front of the Bellenio High School, built in 1956 by the national benefactor Parisis Bellenis. There is a bust of Apostolis Evangelos at the school entrance.

Apostolis Evangelos was born into a poor family on Leros in 1915. He graduated from the High School with top marks and studied at the School of Physics at the University of Athens. When still a student, he visited Leros one day and passed by the headquarters of the governor Bertonelli without greeting him. For this, he was banned from returning to Leros. During the war he fought with the Regiment of the Dodecanesians. He later found himself in Haifa, where he was trained as a commando and wireless transmitter. He was active in Crete, where he was arrested after being betrayed and brutally tortured along with Second Lieutenant Vandoulakis and Colonel Papadakis. He was executed on 23 December 1942.

After the High School playing field, extending as far as Ayia Marina, there begins a neighbourhood full of neo-classical houses. The sense of aristocratic decline in the frayed walls blends with the bourgeois grandeur of the restored buildings, taking you back in time to the great merchants of cosmopolitan Hellenism. Exploration, innovation, the glimmer of the story of ochre and the plaster neo-classical decorative design is here.

The splendid buildings of the Elementary School of Ayia Marina are the living history of education on Leros. After the 1821 War of Independence there was a great need to open community Greek Schools. Thus in 1838, with a bequest from the Lerian Bishop of Bythinia

The Nikolaideios Girls School with the three busts of its patrons, Vasileios Nikolaideios, Theologos Markopoulos and Panayiotis Trakas.

Mitrophanes, the "allilodidaktiko" (a teaching method whereby more able pupils taught the others) school and the Greek School were founded. A Girls School was also opened in 1865 near Ayia Paraskevi. The town's housing development, which had the aesthetic of the large urban centres, could not but leave its mark on the school buildings as well. In 1882, then, the Astike (city) School was built on the site of the "allilodidaktiko" school. A marble inscription in the wall of the restored building, which today houses the Archaeological Museum, reads:

ASTIKE SCHOOL OF LEROS
FOUNDED BY THE LERIAN BROTHERHOOD
OF CAIRO IN THE YEAR 1882

At the same time, the building of the Greek School was erected by the community, and today houses the nursery school. The Nikolaideios Girls School was founded in 1890 by Vasileios Nikolaideios. When he died in Paris, he left a bequest by which the schools would be run and maintained. The neo-classical building still survives today, and is most impressive. There are three busts at the entrance of the school, of the patrons and benefactors of education in Leros - Vasileios Nikolaideios, Theologos Markopoulos and Panayiotis Trakas. The two entrances of the building are made from grey chopped mantoma blocks in the Doric order. The building is painted the colour of ochre, whilst the fluted columns, the cornices and the eaves are white. There are three statues on the peak of the roof, of Athena, Sophia (wisdom) and the muse Calliope, the muse of history. Behind the Girls School stood the Kiosk, which was destroyed by the bombings of the Battle of Leros and which was later, inexplicably, knocked down.

The Malacheio Nursery was built by the patron Theodoros Malachias in 1910-1912. Malachias had been born in Leros in 1857 and migrated at a young age to Egypt. Here he managed to gain control of the sale of fish, fruit and vegetables that he would bring from Kos with his own boat. The original apses are missing from the facade of this building, which today houses the Ayia Marina Elementary School, on a street that still maintains its historical form with its neo-classical buildings.

Panoramic view of Ayia Marina

The Archaeological Museum

The Archaeological Museum is housed in the restored neo-classical building of the old City School, with exhibitions of archaeological finds from excavations and collections. A brief historical overview, details on the island's geographical location, and an account of the mythology of Leros introduce the visitor to the exhibitions. The first section focuses on the prehistory of Leros. Two cases contain finds, pottery and stone tools from the excavation at Kontaris, as well as finds from other prehistoric sites on the islet of Ayios Isidoros, Drymonas, etc.

The second section focuses on the historical era and the political relations of the island with Miletus. Representative pieces of pottery from the geometric until the Roman periods are on display, as well as agnythes (clay loom weights) that were found at Bourtzi. At this site were also found a clay mask of Dionysos, a female bust and a figurine of a symposiast dating to the 4th or 3rd century BC. In this section are provided descriptions of fortifications and decrees from the 3rd and 2nd centuries BC. There follows a thematic unit on cults and sanctuaries, featuring a Roman statuette of the goddess Hygeia. There are also burial offerings, inscribed grave stele, and an inscription mentioning a family funerary monument. In the centre of the exhibition hall is an exhibition of amphorae that have been found in the sea.

The third section focuses on the early Christian period, with an exhibition of finds from the excavation in the early Christian basilica at Partheni, including coins and pieces of wall paintings. The early Christian stone architectural members are placed so as to indicate their positioning on the temple. On the floor are mosaics from the basilicas at Partheni, Ayioi Saranta and Alinda.

The fourth section focuses on the medieval period, featuring the castle of Panteli (the Kastro) and slides with documents from the archive of the Monastery of Patmos that provide valuable information on Leros at the time. Drawings and photographs give a clearer idea of the architecture and painting. The next unit is dedicated to pilgrims and travellers who refer to Leros. In one case there is a pectoral cross with a clay enkolpion (devotional pediment), and talismans from pilgrimages. The final section focuses on the so-called "Milesian islands", with prehistoric pottery and stone tools from the Pharmaco islands, where Julius Caesar had been held captive.

The mosaic floor from the early Christian basilica of Partheni is exhibited outside in the museum yard, along with various architectural members. Exploration of the island should perhaps begin at the museum, which provides a vibrant and well-documented history of the island.

A slip road begins opposite the Elementary School and next to the bed of the river Halikias. Characteristic little stone bridges above the stream unite the entrances of the adjoining mansions with the road. The road leads to

1. Clay figurine of a symposiast, from the locale of Broutzi (late 4th c. BC, Leros Archaeological Museum).
2. Clay mask of Dionysius from the locale of Broutzi (first half 3rd c. BC, Leros Archaeological Museum).
3. Pithos jars (4th-2nd c. BC, Leros Archaeological Museum).

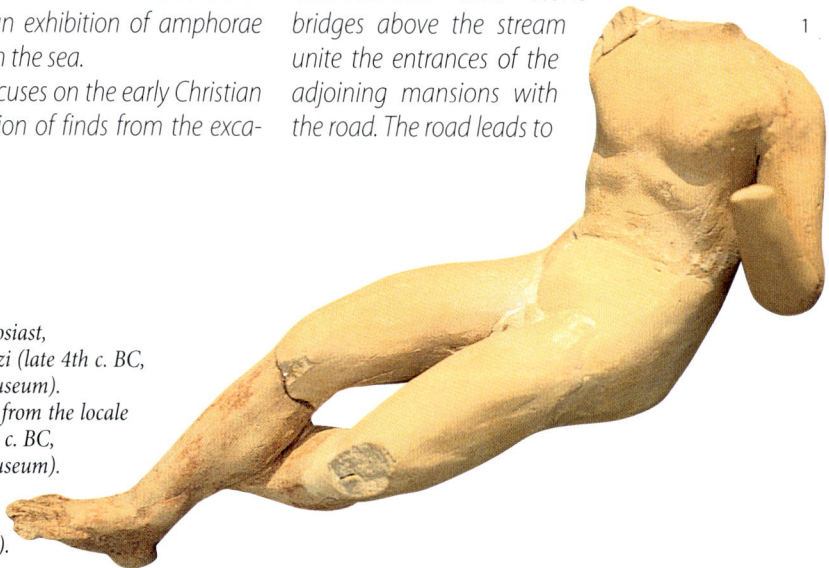

2

3

a small neighbourhood with the neo-classical mansions of Perakis, Mylonas, Haramis and Konstantinides. All built in the early 1880s with round coats of arms in the facades, giving in addition to the initials of the owner the date at which the building was constructed.
A forgotten neighbourhood with the abandoned gardens of the mansions and the half-fallen row of trees. A memory of that golden age when the forgotten Ottoman province was transformed into a miniature copy of the great centres of flourishing Hellenism.

At the end of this road a smaller road to the left leads to the little church of Ayia Varvara, built by Papanastasis over an old cistern.
But the big surprise comes from the area around the church and the remains of an early Christian church, double the length, whilst buried beneath the earth are the seats for the clerics of another basilica that was uncovered by hens from the nearby coops when scraping at the ground. Today they both await the archaeologist's trowel to reveal the secrets of their stone and the historical past of the hamlet of Ayia Marina.

We return to the declining central road, with the old neo-classical mansions of Roussos and Markopoulos to the right and left, and the house of the unforgettable high school principle and historian of the island Michalis Samarkos. The old mansion which today houses municipal services was the headquarters of the German police when they occupied the island. The road narrows at this point, the northerly meltemi wind announces the next scene, and suddenly we see afore us the gulf of Ayia Marina with its port.

The mansion of Perakis.

Ayia Marina

"The columns light their candles,
make the sign of the cross
and behind the fraying walls of the old Customs
House the centurion Prevezis finally appears
playing marching songs of Katy Gray"

The Diproko, D. Kostopoulos

If Platanos is the heart of the island, then Ayia Marina is its senses and its carefree charm, a drop of old wine in the continuous history of the salty sea. Because the port is old, as is its cosmopolitan melancholy.

At Ayia Marina everything is sweetly confused, the Italian buildings with the Greek neo-classical, the fishing boats with the yachts, rock music with the oriental Greek amanades tunes, and the straight blonde hair of northern European beauty with the dark Mediterranean version of passion. The port has its own style that unravels throughout the day, beginning with the outstretched frame of the open-air fish market and ending smothered among the alcohol and the erotic breaches of the mind at night.

The buildings of the old Roussos shipping family dominate the pier, now converted into bars and cafes and, like a pyrgaki that cuts the road in two, into a patisserie. The Italian Customs House, built possibly on a design by Petracco in 1932 and still with the coat of arms of the Italian king (regia dogana), now houses the municipal radio station, Radio Leros on 102.5 FM, on its upper floor, from where the visitor can hear about all the events on the island. Adjacent

1

is the empty building of the Italian Post Office (Posta), with its Italian inscriptions on the post boxes in the walls, encircled by the chairs of the cafes. The Theatre Group is housed on the ground floor of the Customs House, and each summer puts on a theatrical production. In front of the entrance of the Theatre Group, in between two old black cannons and on a paved surface is the bust of Papanastasis.

The priest Anastasio Zafeiropoulos (Papanastasis) was a heroic figure in the resistance against the Italians, who raised the Greek flag from the belfry of the church of Ayia Paraskevi on 4 December 1934. The Italians warned the Mayor and the Bishop that they should lower the flag, otherwise they would bomb the church. Papanastasis rang the bell and a crowd of people gathered in the church. Finally a squad of Carabinieri arrested him and sent him to the prisons at Rhodes on a commercial boat.

Ayia Marina was traditionally the port of Leros, until the Italians developed and used Lakki. Here there was the Customs House, the Post Office and the shipping agency of the Austrian Lloyd Triestino where, funded by the Lerian community of Egypt, the ship running the Alexandria – Smyrna route would run. Yet, the large pier was to be converted into a parking area once noisy nightlife raided the port, and now it houses not only fishing tavernas, but fishing boats, hydrofoils, catamarans, as well as ferries when the sorokada, the strong south-east wind, makes Lakki inhospitable.

1. Panoramic view of Ayia Marina.
2. Greek neo-classical mansion.
3. A view of the beach of Ayia Marina..

The road beyond the pier leads to **Broutzi**, the old fortress that controls the entrance to the port; there are Roman traces, but it was most likely fortified by the Turks. Above, like a hermit on the bare slopes of the mountain, is the building of the old leper colony. We pass the now closed old carnagio of the island, where small boats were repaired, the professions that are being lost, since Giavris preferred the security of running a lottery agency. Next to it, dark and abandoned, is the large building of Kastis's mechanical flour mill, being the first on the island to be steam-powered, closing the windmills. Opposite, on the other side of the port, is the old mill standing in the sea, lit today, it takes its revenge, extolling history's games.

We return to the centre of the island and, in the corner where the road from Platanos leads, we find the storerooms of Tsalikis, with the miniature pediment on an ancient temple on its neo-classical facade. Next to it is the coffee house, tables out and on the road, standing also frozen in time and in the breeze of the meltemi wind. Continuing along the road that slices in between the buildings, we encounter the Italian Bauhaus-style police building, built in 1934-1935 most likely with designs by Petracco and Bernabitti and today home to the Greek Police. Further down are the buildings of the Italian market, built in 1934 most probably with Petracco as architect. A narrow lane leads up some stairs, through the steep neighbourhood streets and tightly packed houses. After a small opening in front of the market, the road is lost between two houses, an old stone mansion, one being of those built from the labours of the sea, as though pinned on to the waves and withstanding all the erosion that it can.

The road continues and, leaving the port behind, meets the central road that leads to Alinda. It is worth taking a stroll on the small paved area that, beneath the road, leads to Myloi. The old neighbourhood beach is unchanged through time, with the patina of colour and the salty sea lying over its traditional houses. Our childhood bathing on the coastline of Attica, stools in the doorways and grandmothers with black underskirts in the sea. And then came the concrete.

The beach of Ayia Marina and, behind, the Kastro.

A little before **Krithoni** two large neo-classical houses stand opposite each other, one restored, the other a ruin, one in cash and one on credit, associative surrealism, the building has its own history. Krithoni, the neighbourhood of the hotels, with the small port and beach beneath the shade of the trees, a little house and Asvestas's old café next to the luxury Crithoni's Paradise.

The central road twists and turns through a series of small gulfs as far as Alinda. The Maratos villa and, high on the hill, Manoelides's villa, someone told me that 2,000 workers rolled cigarettes at his factory in Cairo.

Leros was the diocese of the Bishop of Lerni from Byzantine times until 1888, when the Diocese of Leros and Kalymnos was proclaimed. The Patriarch of Alexandria Sophronios visited Leros in 1882 and was so enthused by the island's climate that he decided to build a summer residence for his holidays. Supervision of the building was the responsibility of the rich merchant Nikolaos Haramis, who hosted him at his villa in Alinda. One and a half years later, the "Patriarchate", as the villa had been named, was ready, along with the church of Ayios Sophronios. The residents welcomed the

Patriarch with the ringing of bells and the burning of an old boat in the Alinda gulf. Sophronios died aged 110.

Today the Patriarchate has been furnished with a conference room. It stands on the edge of the gulf, a lookout or viglator in the sweet fading of the summer that, piled next to the waves, extols the sweet indolent beauty of Alinda. As though the summerhouses of the Lerians of Egypt have inoculated the landscape.

1. The "Patriarchate" with the villa of the Patriarch of Alexandria Sophronios.
2. The beach of Krtihoni.

Alinda - Panayies - Dyo Liskaria

Alinda is the largest and most visited of the island's beaches, with a length of around one kilometre. The lush hills, now full of summerhouses, run down to and then disappear beneath the salty trees of the beach. Alinda was the beloved summer place of the Lerians of Egypt and many of their summer villas, all surrounded by large gardens, still stand today, preserving in a sense the charm of Alinda and preventing the invasion of the gluttonous model of tourism that builds right on the beach. Despite all this, Alinda in the summer is like a colourful fair right next to the waves, lasting until sunset.

Then they light their little lamps, take out their tables, right opposite Ayia Marina with the lit castle, and it is transformed into a small gourmand feast, to a sacred place of the summer party of friends, immortal throughout the centuries. The type of party that only the tiny islands of the archipelago know how to attract and to scatter with the first drops of rain.

1. *Scene of Alnida nightlife.*
2. *Preparations for the "Alindia", the popular Water Sports Games.*
3. *Beach and fishing boats.*

The powerful charm of the name Alinda seeks it etymology in the verb alindo = to turn, although its historical origin is probably much earlier. Opposite, on the Asia Minor coast of the gulf of Gerondas, there stood an ancient Greek city of Alinda, with a strong fortress. Alinda later became a diocese, and its Bishops were given honourable mention at many early church synods, the last being the Ecumenical Synod of Constantinople in 883, at which Theophilos Bishop of Alinda participated. Suddenly, from that point on the city is not mentioned again, not even at the next Ecumenical Synod in 887. It is likely, then, that the Alinda of Caria was destroyed by a natural disaster or a raid, and its inhabitants relocated to the nearest opposite island, which was Leros. It is indeed very possible that they chose to settle in the gulf of Alinda opposite Caria, which could be seen on a clear day. Naturally they gave its name to their new home.

On the left of the road, immediately after the Patriarchate, is the British cemetery with the uniform white graves standing on the grass. These are the graves of the British soldiers killed on the island in November 1943 during the Battle of Leros. After heavy bombardments for around two months, around 3,000 German commandos and parachutists bent the resistance of around 3,000 British soldiers and 8,000 of the former German allies, the Italians, finally occupying the island. The Battle of Leros was one of the most important throughout the Second World War, and the Germans' last victory before their collapse.

On the tombstones can be seen, in addition to the names (although many were never recognised), the symbols of the British units. The King's Own, the Buffs, the RIF (the Royal Irish Fusiliers) all buried next to their comrades.

Continuing along the beach, noisy in the summer yet almost deserted in the winter, it is worth taking a stop at the old Municipal Hostel. Here, in the area of the outdoor restaurant the history that chases your every step through the island is revealed in the marble floor of the 6th-century early Christian church, surrounded

by railings. At the hostel it is worth tasting the home-cooked food of Kyra Virginia. A small road after the hostel leads up amongst some laurel trees – a piece of the atmosphere of the old Alinda surviving a few metres from the beach – leads to the church of the Ayioi Saranda. The mosaics from an early Christian church found in the yard have now been moved to the Archaeological Museum. Returning along the same road, we encounter the villa of Haramis on the beach. The external form of this old building has been changed, but inside it is as it was, with portraits of the wealthy merchant Nikolaos Haramis and his brother Adamantios.

Adamantios Haramis was born in Leros on 26 September 1830, completing his basic education here. He continued his High School and University studies in Athens, moving to Russia on graduation, where there was a large Greek merchant community, as a teacher to the Scaramangas family. There he later became Head of the local Greek school, maintaining close relations with Paris, which he visited regularly, and with intellectual figures of his era – he was a personal friend of the German philosopher Hegel. Haramis translated Pushkin into Greek, although this was published posthumously by his brother Nikolaos. He returned to Leros during the last years of his life, where he met the historian Karl Krumbacher, who was impressed by his garden and library. The library is today to be found in the Municipal Library at Platano, whilst only two trees are remaining from Haramis's garden. Haramis died in the old villa on 6 February 1885 at the age of 55.

1. Grave goods from the site of Sykies at Alinda, late 5th c. BC.
2. Perfume jars of the "bulbous" type, 1st c. BC – 1st c. AD.
3. Panoramic view of Alinda.

A few metres further down we encounter the **tower of Bellenis**, built in a medieval style in 1925-26. It has been characterised as a listed monument and work of art by the Ministry of Culture. It came under the responsibility of the Municipality of Leros in the early 1980s and is now restored and home to the Manolis Isychos Museum, in honour of the Museum's founder Manolis Isychos, who was also the first director of the Regional Archive.

The tower's basement and first floor house the **Folk Museum**, which has a collection emanating from the traditional culture of Leros, including handicrafts, vessels, furniture, costume and musical instruments. The Tsakiri Room is also to be found on the first floor, with works by this political prisoner who was held captive at Partheni in 1967-1973, during the days of the military junta. Painted stones, canvases and coal sketches for the wall paintings at Ayia Kioura. There are also exhibits from the old Community Pharmacy and the old printing presses from the Royal Technical Schools, where the first Lerian publications were produced.

The **Historical Museum** is on the first floor, with photographs and military exhibits from the Battle of Leros and the destroyer the Queen Olga. Finally, the second floor has an exhibition room with works by Lerian painters, whilst the Bellenis Hall has the photographs and personal effects of Parisis Bellenis.

Parisis Bellenis was born in Leros in 1871, moving to Cairo at a young age, where he worked hard in the Lerian businesses of Egypt. He quickly developed into a contractor for large projects and almost had a monopoly on the works of the Egyptian government as well as British companies. He learnt to speak four languages and was a personal friend of the Greek Prime Minister Eleftherios Venizelos, who commissioned him to build and supervise public works in Eastern Thrace. He was the president of both the Lerian Brotherhood and the Greek community of Cairo for many years. The shooting range near the columns of the temple of Olympian Zeus in Athens were built with his donation, and were opened in 1908 by Crown Prince Constantine. In Leros, in addition to the pyrgos he also built the High School. He died in 1957 and was proclaimed as a National Benefactor by the Greek state.

The road continues after the tower among a myriad of shops, restaurants, supermarkets, cafes and bars, as far as the edge of the gulf, where the coast, in front of an old oil press that has left a consignment of aromas, has been converted into a mooring place for boats. This is where the commercial tourism activity ends and the road, beneath the shade of a eucalyptus

tree, reaches as far as Panayies at the point where there used to be an early Christian church with a beautiful stone yard and wondrous view towards the castle.

A pretty bay spreads out beneath the church, drowning in green, whilst on the seabed are the remains of a German landing boat that, ablaze under running fire, managed to land its men. In October 2003 a Junker 52 was pulled out of the gulf of Ayia Marina, which had been hit and fallen in November 1943 after dropping off parachutists at Rachi during the Battle of Leros. Who can today imagine that magical Alinda had been the scene of a fierce hand to hand battle 60 years earlier.

Continuing, we reach the beach of **Dyo Liska-ria.** The opening first and later the surfacing of the road have transformed this deserted old beach, from a nudist refuge to a busy beach with a restaurant and bar, particularly pretty and quiet at night, like a glow-worm in the dark.

One can reach **Kryfos** by walking over the spine of the mountain, although the most usual means is by boat. This is a small cape in amongst the rocks, with a cave and a refreshing spring. The capes of Pano and Kato Zymi on the barren side of the island, wild and beaten by the wind, have a historical value. Here at Pano Zymi the Germans, despite the loss of two landing boats, were able to anchor and penetrate as far as Kryfos, where they apprehended two small Italian vessels. Above the mountain massif of Kleidion, occupied by the Ciano Battery, stands tall. The Battery installations, taken by the Germans in a fierce battle, are still standing today, and access is not prohibited. The Italian officers were executed on the spot by the Germans and the grave of one of them lies in the Italian cemetery at Temenia.

1. The tower of Bellenis.
2, 3. Rooms in the Manolis Isychos Museum.
4. Panoramic view of the beach of Dyo Liskaria.

4

Alinda - Ayios Isidoros - Partheni - Plefoutis

The central road at the beginning of Alinda beach turns to the left, leaving the small copse on the right and heads towards Partheni. Of the German cemetery that lay once in the copse only the base of a cross now remains. A few metres further along, at a crossing in a small square, the road to the left leads to **Gourna** and **Rachi**.

Continuing towards the area of Kamara ("arch"), which may have taken its name from the domed structure that stood there, a small road to the left leads to **Kokalli** (1 km) and Ayios Isidoros. Kokkali, a small, quiet country place with clear but cold waters and underwater streams. The "residence" of Zaphiris was at Kokkali, where they hid the allied wireless radio during the German occupation, along with the Chiot wireless operator Mavrogiorgis (the pseudonym of Antonis Filamis). A little further down a dirt track leads to the Pontikonisi of Leros. The **little church of Ayios Isidoros** is built on a rocky islet in the gulf of Kokkali, which you can reach via a surfaced footpath when the weather is good. The charm of this maritime desert breathes relaxed, whilst within the waters the foundations of an early Christian church under siege from the sea-urchins, can be seen.

We return to the central road lined with eucalyptus trees and the old Italian storerooms to the right and the left, and reach the dyke. Going by the indications on the wettest days when it fills with birds, if ever it were to operate then this dyke would create an impressive small wetland. A little before the dyke a dirt road leads to **Ayios Nikolas at Meraloudis**, with a small deserted beach. It is said that the small church where they once celebrated Easter in the middle of winter, was built by a foreign captain who nearly drowned in those parts, hence he ordered the church to be built.

A dirt road immediately after the dyke leads to the ruins of an ancient fortress, which until recently was believed to belong to the temple of Artemis.

It is built like that of Paliokastro at Xerokampos, with regular stone blocks and with the pseudo-isodomic system, since each joint between two blocks does not terminate precisely in the centre of the lower one. It is believed that there stood an ancient signalling station on the inner side of the wall. There is a little Byzantine church two hundred or so metres from the small fortress. It might even be these cyclamens, sprouting out from the deep historical heritage of the stone, which were turned into a song by the renowned composer Mikis Theodorakis.

The dirt road continues towards Ayios Yiannis at Fakoudia, there where there had been an early Christian church and the installations of the 906th Battery at Moblogourna. Even though the signs of the explosions are clear, the bases of the cannons and the barracks with the inscription "deo – patria –rex". i.e. "God – Country – King" in the entrance can still be seen. Inside, the German wall paintings with the planes coexist with

the rods of the faccio and the aspiration of the inscription, for death in battle for the motherland: "voglio morire in combattimento che morire senza rivodere la patria".

Further to the right at Markello is the Battery Farinata, with its semi-ruined headquarters and, of course, a sheep pen as in all the military installations in the mountains. The most impressive and well-preserved structure is the lookout post, which is reminiscent of a submarine periscope.

We return to the central road and the airport. A brief archaeological excavation was conducted in 1980, during works for the construction of the airport, before the new airport could put a final end to such searches.

1. The little church of Ayios Isidoros.
2. The beach of Ayios Nikolaos at Meraloudis.
3. The gulf of Kokkalis with Ayios Isidoros.

A Roman building complex was discovered, perhaps a forum the existence of which continued into early Christian times. Nine burials and the remains of an early Christian basilica were also found. The basilica experienced two building phases, with three aisles until the end of the 5th century and as a smaller long and narrow one until the end of the 6th century. The mosaic floor of the later church, with geometric designs and inscriptions, is now in the Archaeological Museum. This was probably also the site of the temple of Parthenos Artemis, architectural members of which may have been used in the construction of the Christian basilica. Indeed, the name of the town Partheni goes back to that of the goddess, as areas with sanctuaries of the Parthenos ("virgin") were called "parthenia".

After the airport the leeward gulf of Partheni spreads out before us, with the island of **Archangelos** acting as a bar that protects it from the easterly winds. It is said that the port of Partheni could comfortably hold 700 ships and still not be visible from the sea. The old ship owners would moor their two- and three-masted ships here from the middle of December until the middle of January, waiting for the asperges of the waters. It is also said that the naval hero of the Greek War of Independence Andreas Miaoulis, when hunted by Turkish boats, found refuge in Partheni behind Archangelos. The Turks bypassed Archangelos without imagining where he had hidden, and continued their pursuit in the empty sea. Archangelos, which can be visited from Partheni in small boats, has wonderful sandy beaches. There are many fish farms and installations for keeping and maintaining ships at Partheni.

Partheni was the first place that the Italians fortified, with old cannons brought over from Libya. It is from here that the campaign against the Dardanelles began. The David Diamantaras military camp is the old Italian camp, with the headquarters still preserved almost untouched. In front of the storerooms, which today have a different purpose, the rails for the wagons that transported military materials, torpedoes and mines to the port can be seen. It was to these storerooms that many of the political prisoners of the April 1967 military coup were brought. Indeed, the road in front of the military camp is today called "Odos Politikon Kratoumenon" (Political Prisoners Street). Among the many prisoners, Mikis Theodorakis, the poet Yiannis Ritsos and the politicians Manolis Glezos and Harilaos Florides were also interned here. In these storerooms, where the entire leadership of the Greek Communist Party was held, the historic communist split took place. Every summer the "Celebration of Memory and Democracy" is held, with a memorial service.

After the military camp there is a fork in the road. One turning leads after 800 metres to Ayia Kioura, whilst the other again after 800 metres leads to the beach of Plefoutis. Both roads have an asphalt surface.

The road for Ayia Kioura passes by the small **lake of Rina**. This is where the Italian refrigerator-ship the Ivorea had sought refuge in October 1943 after the bombardments, but it was discovered by German planes, which sunk it. A small section escaped disintegration and remains half-sunken in the waters. There are also the remains of the net that blocked the submarines, the bollards of the ships, and thrown in one corner is the buoy that held the net and the floors of the Italian hangars and storerooms.

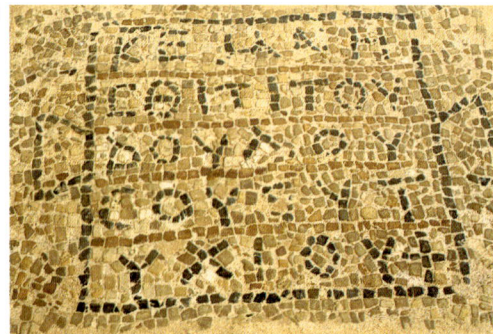

1. Mosaic dedicatory inscription from the early Christian church at Partheni (4th c. BC, Leros Archaeological Museum).
2. The little lake of Rina.
3. Remains of the early Christian basilica at Partheni.

Ayia Kioura

"…is situated the site of Ayia Kioura, called thus after a chapel there that was named in honour of Ayia Matroni, who in Greek was called Ayia Kyra (Lady) and with the –u of the Attic dialect Ayia Kioura."

Leriaka, *1888, D. Oikonomopoulos*

The Byzantine church of Ayia Kioura is located on the site of an early Christian church, and has been pronounced a historic monument. Inside it there is an impressive icon of Ayia Matrona the Chiopoitissa, with a silver-plated halo and two inscriptions at the foot: "1786 by Nikolaos Reginas" and "with the donations of the Gemicides, in memory Lord". Persecuted by the Turks, many Chiots came to Leros in the 18th century. They erected the church of Ayia Matrona, and the gemici, as the sailors were known, dedicated the famous icon to the church.

During the military dictatorship, the painter Kyriakos Tsakiris was one of the many exiled to Partheni. In 1971 the internees proposed to the director of the camp, who was named Spyrakis, that they paint icons in the church. Spyrakis was a religious man and he accepted their proposal, helping to collect a little money to buy the materials. He also provided guards to help the prisoners. The work was undertaken by Kyriakos Tsakiris along with the other painter-prisoners, Antonis Karayiannis and Takis Tzaneteas. The icon painting lasted for eight months, and the three painters worked ten hours a day, many times working at night with fog lamps. They used other prisoners, local residents and even prison guards as their models. The model for one of the Apostles is now a priest on the island, Papa Maximos, and the daughter of a taverna owner was the Virgin Mary. They painted 38 scenes in total. In the early 1980s, however, a crazy monk who called himself an Abbot and who lived in the hut at the entrance, whitewashed most of them, believing that the representation of the faces of lay people is an act of irreverence. Despite this, the Ministry of Culture pronounced the church to be a preserved and historic monument in 1983.

Kyriakos Tsakiris was born in Asia Minor but grew up in Piraeus. He was a student at Athens University Law School when Greek dictator Metaxas exiled him to Sikinos, where he remained until 1941. He took part in the National Resistance and the ensuing civil war. He was later arrested and took part in the great escape from Vourla. He left prison on 21 April 1966, and exactly one year later, as his wife relates, he returned home all smiles so that they could celebrate a year of freedom together. But, on the night of 21 April 1967, he was again

arrested in the military coup and taken to Leros, from where he was freed in 1972. Exhibitions with his works have been held throughout Greece. In 1974 he was honoured with the State Prize for Literature in the "Witnesses-Chronicles" category. Works by Tsakiris are today on show at the tower of Bellenis, in a special gallery that has been designed in his honour. The pad with his sketchings for the icons on the walls of the church is now in the Regional Archive at Platanos.

In the church of Ayia Kioura one can see the icons painted by the internees of the military dictatorship.

Plefoutis

Returning along the road to the right of the military camp, we are led towards **Plefoutis**, which springs out from high at our feet, with its big beach and the islet of **Strongyli** that protects it from the winds. At the height are the remains of the Italian 888th Battery. The name Plefoutis probably comes from Polyfytis ("many plants"), and many accounts from the previous century describe a far thicker vegetation than today. With the shortening of the Attic dialect, with which many people still speak today, the –u became Plofoutis, and it is still pronounced thus by many people. There is also a restaurant on the beach. At the end of the asphalt road, at the point where the dirt road starts, the beach is full or broken ceramics. This is the area known as Kaminia, with the old ceramics works half-sunken in the sea. A small spring in the sea next to the gulf has a name that describes both its content and the result, "tsirlonero" ("running water").

Continuing along the dirt road we reach **Asfourngaro** and the impressive installations of the 889th Battery. The bases of cannons, barbed wire trenches, and the barracks down below. Again the smell of manure, the puzzled look of the goats and, behind the entrance arches, the frayed walls sing a eulogy to military vanity: "Siamo orgogliosi di occupare un posto di combattimento, di sacrifici e di dovere" (We are proud to be in position for battle, sacrifice and duty"). The wind whistles above the empty lookout post, and beneath the giant limestone mountain massif the sand is whitened by the small harbour of Vagia. Here on the night of 12 November five German landing boats attempted to enter the small cape, but they were hit by the coastal batteries. One boat was sunk and can today be found at a depth of six metres in front of the island of Strongyli. The German commandoes that survived swam as far as Strongyli, where they were arrested by the Italians.

7TH ROUTE

Alinda - Gourna - Drymonas - Ayios Theologos

We take a left at the small, walled square with the crossing at Alinda. These roads cross the western and most fertile part of the island, protected from the winds. A signpost indicates the directions and the distances: Rachi 3 km, Ankyra 4 km, Lakki 5 km. We take the road towards Gourna, a large downward sloping gulf with very shallow waters and sand. When the rain waters flood it in the winter it is reminiscent of a gourna (basin), thus justifying its name.

Driving carefully along the road, the little medieval tower of Gourna can be seen on the left, a few metres off the road. Only the north and west walls are still upright. The south wall is damaged whilst the eastern has completely collapsed. Only a few of the wooden traves and jagged ramparts remain on the roof. The cauldron installation is to be found in excellent condition in the north part. Inside the ground floor the fireplace still exists, with storage cavities in the walls. Continuing our route, we bypass the contemporary imitation of the Caserma Regina and go in the direction of verdant **Drymonas**. A turning on the left that goes through the houses leads to the shore of Drymonas, a quiet area of the island with fresh fish. The road ends at a small Byzantine church of Ayios Georgios that is built in the rock. Inside, the shadows of the saints' paintings can be seen on the walls.

We return to the central road and look for the Byzantine church of the **Panayia Gourlomata**, with the characteristic wall paintings and eyes of the Virgin, on the slope. Built in the 14th century with material from an adjoining older building. The central road continues upwards after Drymonas to the region of Plaka, for which we turn right and continue towards the Panayia Monastery.

To the left of the central road at a distance of 1 km is the area of **Myloi** (mills), with the remains of old mills. The road begins to lead down towards

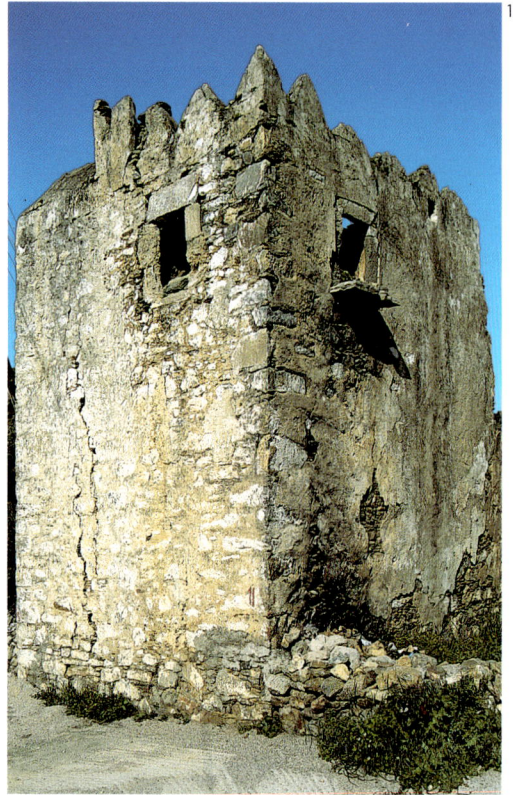

Lakki, with a panoramic view of it from up above. Passing through orchards with neo-classical mansions we reach the church of Ayios Ioannis Theologos. This is the only church surviving in a true Byzantine style on Leros. It was likely built by the Blessed Christodoulos in the 11th century, during his stay in Leros and before he left for Patmos. Materials from the early Christian church that is found on the same site have been incorporated into today's church, which was built over the old Byzantine one by Theologos Markopoulos, a benefactor of the island. Repairs being currently undertaken are expected to reveal new details, covered wall paintings, burials, a skull with injuries from an arrow point, etc. The researchers' final scientific analysis is eagerly awaited, to reveal new light on the island's historical development.

Near the church, in between the districts of **Vayia** and **Ayios Theologos**, right next to the road, is the medieval pyrgospito (tower house) of Vayia. This pyrgospito is of great interest, despite the fact that two of its sides, the south and west, have completely collapsed. The east wall is still preserved in an excellent condition, and has two twin windows with grey mantomata. Right above the windows on the outer wall can be seen, either carved or in relief, two strange designs with rectangular forms and peaked apses alongside birds and trees.

The windows on the inner wall have arches with decorative designs, whilst a carved vase with flowers can be seen on the north wall. Among the detritus the hearth of the fireplace can be made out.

In the south-east corner there is a cross in relief, whilst above it there survives a plank of wood with an opening at its centre. This was most probably the corner where the millstones for the grinding were kept, whilst next to a water basin there is a rifle locker.

The road continues downwards after Ayios Theologos, and passing in front of the PIKPA (Caserma Regina) we reach the circular Roussos Square in Lakki.

1. View from the medieval tower house at Gourna.
2. The beach of Gourna.
3. The Panayia Gourlomata (13th-14th c.) after restoration.

Transport

Leros is 175 miles from Piraeus, and there are daily ferryboat connections via the Piraeus-Patmos-Leros-Kalymnos-Kos-Rhodes route. Journey time is between eight and eleven hours, according to the type of boat. There are also daily flights to the island from Athens in 50-seater planes, with a journey time of 45 minutes. There are flights to the island from Rhodes, Kos and Astypalaia three times a week. A small caique boat runs a daily connection between Leros and Kalymnos, setting out from Xerokampos in the morning and returning in the early afternoon. There is also a caique connection between Leros and the island of Lipsi.

Extra connections are put on in the summer season, with usually two boats a day from Piraeus. There is a great demand for seats on the flights, and you should reserve a place several days in advance. There are also daily connections with hydrofoils ("dolphins") and catamarans, 2-3 connections a day with Kos, Kalymnos, Lipsi, Patmos, Agathonisi, Ikaria, Fournoi and Samos.

Useful telephone numbers

Leros area code: 22470

Olympic Airlines: The Olympic Airlines offices are at Platanos (tel. 22844) and the airport at Partheni (tel. 22777).

Port Authority: The Port Authority is housed in an old neo-classical building at Lakki, a little further up from the Queen Olga monument (tel. 22224).

Taxis: There are three taxi ranks, at Platanos, Lakki and Ayia Marina. There are always taxis waiting at the port and the airport during boat and flight arrivals (tel. 22550- 23070).

Police: The police station is located at Ayia Marina (tel. 22222-3).

Hospital: There is a large hospital at Lakki covering almost all specialisations, with overnight stays and an ambulance always at the ready (tel. 23251).

Town Hall: The Town Hall is to be found at Platanos, whilst many of its services are housed in an old neo-classical building on the road that connects Platanos with Ayia Marina (tel. 22255).

Camping: Outdoor camping is prohibited, but there is an organised campsite at Xerokampos, at the entrance to the village (tel. 22236).

Boat tickets: The agencies that issue boat tickets are located at Lakki. Tickets can also be bought at the port one hour before the boat departure time.

Tickets for hydrofoils can be bought at Ayia Marina (tel. 24110, 22140).

Newspapers - Magazines: There are two newsagents that sell Greek and foreign newspapers and magazines, at Platanos and Ayia Marina. There is also a newspaper sales point at Alinda during the summer.

Banks: There are two branches of the National Bank (Ethniki Trapeza) at Lakki (tel. 23583). There is an Agricultural Bank (Agrotiki) at Ayia Marina (tel. 23234), an Emporiki Bank at Lakki (tel. 25780), as well as an Alpha Bank at Lakki (tel. 26011).

Post Office: The Post Office is on the road that leads out from Platanos to Ayia Marina.

There is also a sub-branch at Lakki (22470 85400).

Museums of Leros

1. Archaeological Museum
This is at Ayia Marina, with a collection that includes inscriptions, small ancient objects, figurines, early Christian artefacts, etc.

2. Manolis Isychos Museum
Located in the tower of Bellenis at Alinda, and includes a folk museum and a history museum.

3. Ecclesiastical Museum
Located in the Panayia tou Kastrou, with vestments, icons, vessels and rare books.

4. General State Archives
– Regional Archive of Leros
At Platanos, with a fine historical archive.

PRIVATE MUSEUMS
1. Mansions of Kandioglou and Antonellos
Located at Platanos and with wonderful interior decoration, the mansions are preserved unchanged, with their furnishings as they were in the old days.

2 . Yiannis Paraponiaris and Tasos Kanaris collections
Private collections with a huge amount of material, photographs, weapons, artefacts, etc, from the Italian period and the Battle of Leros.

Text: DIMITRIS KOSTOPOULOS
Editor: DIMITRIS ANANIADIS
Translation: DESPINA CHRISTODOULOU
Design: EVI DAMIRI
Layout: RANIA TSILOGIANNOPOULOU
Photographs: M. TOUBIS S. A. ARCHIVE, NIKOS DALOGLOU

Pictures have been taken from the book of the Elementary School
of Ayia Marina, Στα Ίχνη της Αρχιτεκτονικής μας Κληρονομιάς,
an edition of the Municipal Cultural Centre of Leros.

Colour Separation – Printing: M. TOUBIS S. A.